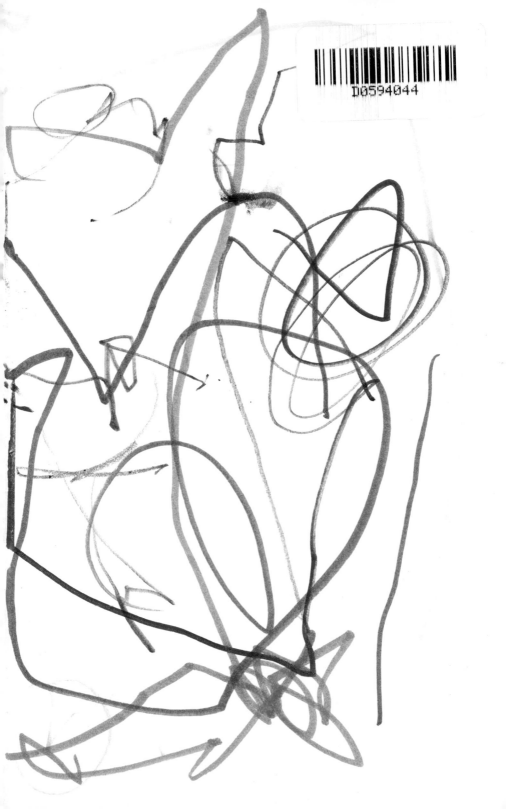

BEWARE! THE LIES OF SATAN

BEWARE! THE LIES OF SATAN

by
Frederick K.C. Price, Ph.D.

FAITH ONE
PUBLISHING
LOS ANGELES, CALIFORNIA

Beware! The Lies of Satan
ISBN 1-883798-16-7 (Soft-cover edition)
ISBN 1-883798-08-6 (Hard-cover edition)
Copyright © 1995 by
Frederick K.C. Price, Ph.D.
P.O. Box 90000
Los Angeles, CA 90009

Published by Faith One Publishing
7901 South Vermont Avenue
Los Angeles, California 90044

Contents

Introduction

People are being lied to every day, and some of them are going to hell because of it! Other people, who are saved and are supposedly children of God, are suffering from illness, poverty, worry, and guilt. Still more are saved and are relatively successful in life. However, if you looked at their lifestyles, you would find it hard to believe they were really born-again, because they are living the same lifestyle as many sinners do, or worse.

The worst part of it is that all of these people think they are supposed to be where they are in their lives, spiritually, physically, mentally, economically, and materially. They do not know that they have gotten the short end of the stick. They do not know they have been lied to and cheated out of what is rightfully theirs. They have been innocent, and, at the same time, ignorant. According to Hosea 4:6, ignorance can kill.

So who has been doing the lying all this time? Who can we pin the blame on? Not the preacher, the deacon, the elder, the seminary, or the Sunday school teacher. They may have passed down false information, but bless their hearts, they were just as sincere as they could be, and probably believed in their hearts that what they were telling everyone else was right. They did not know what they were teaching and preaching was not true or scriptural. They were simply deceived.

You cannot say the world lied, either — not sinners, or the government, or the movies, or the television networks, or the newspapers. The reason is the
same. They were, and are, as deceived as anyone else.
They have been groping in the dark.

So who has been lying, and making everyone suffer
all this time? Take a quick look at the title on the cover of
this book. That will tell you who is responsible.

In case you are thinking or have been told, "That
cannot be true. The devil does not exist," well, according
to the Bible, not only does he exist, but he and his demon
forces are on the rampage today. As Jesus put it, he is
searching the land like a roaring lion, seeking whom he
may devour.

In this book, we will look at who Satan is, where he
came from, and how you can stand in victory over him.
We will look at some of the misconceptions which have
been perpetuated over the years. We will discuss how
Jesus has given us freedom over every negative circum-
stance that can come into our lives, and how we can and
are expected to live in this freedom. We have done nothing to earn this freedom nor can we. It is given to us
when we accept Jesus as our personal Savior and Lord,
because the Heavenly Father loves each of us so much
that He wants us to be happy, successful, and taken-care-
of. You probably want your children to succeed in life, be
joyful, be in good health. Why should God the Father be
any different?

The answer is that God is not any different, despite
what you may have thought or heard. It is not my opinion. It is what the Bible tells us, in black and white. God
says in His Word that He does not change, nor has He

any shadow of turning. That means His promises do not change, either. If we want to know God's nature, what He has done for us, what He is willing to do for us even now, and what is not true about Him, all we have to do is look at what He says in His Word, and go from there.

This book is not an end, but a beginning, a start in discovering answers to some age-old questions. The rest is up to us.

The Apostle Paul says in 2 Tim. 2:15, **Be diligent to present yourself approved to God, a workman who does not need to be ashamed, rightly dividing the word of truth.** That means the ball is in our court to get to know God. My wish is that this book will encourage you to do so, as well as encourage you to live the overcoming Christian life that Christ has bought and paid for, for us.

Lie 1
There Is No Personal Devil

I have heard people say, "There is no personal devil. The idea of a devil is simply a state of mind, conceptualized by religionists to cause us fear." In society, we have made a cartoon character out of him, complete with red suit, long tail, pitchfork, and horns. When we see him displayed in the movies or on television, he is made out to be some sort of joke, a wimp who cannot hold his own against human ingenuity when push comes to shove.

According to the Bible, the devil is not a wimp, and he is anything but a joke. The Word says he is a thief, a killer, a robber, a roaring lion seeking whom he may devour. Just as the Holy Spirit is described in the Bible in terms that denote his function (i.e., the Helper, the Comforter, the teacher, the Spirit of truth), so Satan is described in the Scriptures by the names that describe what he has done and is doing in the earth realm today. And it all spells bad news!

The Bible tells us the devil is real, that he exists. Unfortunately, he is also winning far too many battles when it comes to the family of God. Hosea 4:6 says, **My people are destroyed for lack of knowledge.** That includes not only knowledge about the devil's existence, but also the fact that you can stop him from lording it over you.

The first thing we need to do is establish from the Word of God the origin of this personage. That way, we can know as much as possible about our chief adversary. By knowing where he came from and how he operates, we can have a clearer understanding of his modus operandi.

How Satan Became Satan

We have two excellent descriptions in the Old Testament of what Satan was like in the beginning and what prompted his becoming what he is today. Together, they form a very interesting composite of the enemy we face. The first of these descriptions is found in Isaiah 14:12-15:

> "How you are fallen from heaven,
> O Lucifer, son of the morning!
> How you are cut down to the ground,
> You who weakened the nations!
> For you have said in your heart:
> 'I will ascend into heaven,
> I will exalt my throne above the stars of God;
> I will also sit on the mount of the congregation
> On the farthest sides of the north;
> I will ascend above the heights of the clouds,
> I will be like the Most High.'
> Yet you shall be brought down to Sheol,
> To the lowest depths of the Pit."

Lucifer was Satan's technical or given name when he was created. He is not a human creature, but a heavenly creature. He did not fall from earth. He fell from heaven.

We find out more about Lucifer in Ezekiel 28:11-17:

> Moreover the word of the Lord came to me, saying, "Son of man, take up a lamentation for the king of Tyre, and say to him, 'Thus says the Lord God:
>
> "You were the seal of perfection,
> Full of wisdom and perfect in beauty.
> You were in Eden, the garden of God;
> Every precious stone was your covering:
> The sardius, topaz, and diamond,
> Beryl, onyx, and jasper,
> Sapphire, turquoise, and emerald with gold.
> The workmanship of your timbrels and pipes
> Was prepared for you on the day you were created.
>
> "You were the anointed cherub who covers;
> I established you;
> You were on the holy mountain of God;
> You walked back and forth in the midst of fiery stones.
> You were perfect in your ways from the day you were created,
> Till iniquity was found in you.
>
> "By the abundance of your trading
> You became filled with violence within,
> And you sinned;
> Therefore I cast you as a profane thing
> Out of the mountain of God;
> And I destroyed you, O covering cherub,
> From the midst of the fiery stones.

[A cherub is an angel, not a man. He is not an earthly king, but a supernatural creature, one beyond the realm of flesh and blood.]

> "Your heart was lifted up because of your beauty;
> You corrupted your wisdom for the sake of your splendor;
> I cast you to the ground,
> I laid you before kings,
> That they might gaze at you."

As I said before, these two descriptions of Satan form a composite sketch of where this angelic creature came from, what his purpose was in the beginning, and how he became what he is today. Even with this sketch, however, there are some gaps in continuity.

In the Beginning?

What I am about to say may not seem related at first to the subject at hand, but bear with me. As I will show later in this book, it is directly related. When you read Genesis 1:1 in the King James Bible, it says, **In the beginning....** Literally, in the Hebrew, this verse begins, "In beginning ..." However, verse two adds, **The earth was without form, and void....**

Why would God create something without form and void? That in itself would seem to contradict what He says in Isaiah 45:18:

4

> For thus says the Lord,
> Who created the heavens,
> Who is God,
> Who formed the earth and made it,
> Who has established it,
> Who did not create it in vain,
> Who formed it to be inhabited:
> "I am the Lord, and there is no other."

The words *not in vain*, in the Hebrew, literally mean "not without form." In fact, one translation of this verse says that God did not create the earth as a formless waste. Yet that is what is being described in Genesis 1:2. Also, Genesis 1:2 says, ... **and darkness was on the face of the deep.** Literally, in the Hebrew, it says there was chaos. God does not create chaos, because chaos is confusion, and the Bible says God is not the author of confusion.

Why would God create a world, submerge it in water, then call the ground to come up out of the water to form continents and islands? The Spirit of the Lord gave me what I believe to be the answer to this question, and it ties directly into the origin of Satan. If you have a challenge with it, you do not have to accept it. After all, your salvation is not based on what I am about to say.

I believe that when God created this world initially, Satan (the bright star, Lucifer) was placed in charge of this earth realm, and his job was to bring the praise, worship, and adoration of the creatures of the earth to God. Lucifer was a very beautiful angel; in fact, he was the most beautiful angel God had created. However, because of his beauty, his pride got in the way.

Lucifer thought that since he was so beautiful, the praise and adoration of these creatures should be directed to him. He said, "I will exalt my throne above the throne of God." He became perverted, and as a result of his actions, not only himself, but the whole earth was plunged into a chaotic condition.

Actually, Genesis 1:2 to the end of that chapter is really not the story of creation. It is the story of the restoration of this earth out of the chaos that resulted from Satan's rebellion against God. If you read that chapter carefully, you will notice that everything in this earth realm was plunged into darkness. When God originally created the earth, He did not create it in darkness, because the Bible says that God is light, and that in Him is no darkness at all.

Of course, we have to account for the dinosaurs and all that went with them. I will agree there are many discrepancies in history concerning the so-called "cave men." There is some fabrication which has been proved, and some lies told to try to perpetuate the idea that man evolved from a less advanced species. However, archaeologists did not fabricate the bones they have unearthed over the years — the bones of animals that they say predate the Garden of Eden. The Bible time clock indicates that the time period from the Garden of Eden to now is approximately 6,000 years — 4,000 years from Adam to Christ, and approximately another 2,000 years from Christ to this present time. According to these scientists, the bones they have discovered predate the Bible time clock by many thousands of years.

In the last 6,000 years of recorded history, there have been no such animals as Tyrannosaurus Rex,

Apatosaurus (formerly Brontosaurus), or any other dinosaurs living on the earth. However, those bones had to come from somewhere. I believe they are the bones of animals that existed in the pre-Adamic earth before it was plunged into chaos as a result of this spirit creature, Satan. These animals were destroyed, along with everything else on this planet, because of Satan's sin.

Access From the Heavenlies

The Bible refers to three heavens. (There is no such thing in the Bible as seven heavens.) The atmosphere around this earth, otherwise known as the firmament, is the first heaven. The heaven where God the Father dwells, where His throne and the golden city are located, is referred to as the third heaven. In between the first heaven and the third heaven is what is referred to in the Bible as the heavenlies.

The best way to picture this is to imagine a salami sandwich — two pieces of bread and one piece of salami. The salami is in between both pieces of bread, touching both sides, yet is a separate entity in itself. Think of the top slice of bread as the third heaven, the salami as the heavenlies, and the bottom slice of bread as the heaven that surrounds the earth.

When Satan was cast down from his position as bright star or son of the morning, he was cast out of the third heaven, and cast into the heavenlies. From the heavenlies, Satan has access to the earth-realm, and, as Job 1:6 shows us, also to the third heaven.

> Now there was a day when the sons of God came
> to present themselves before the Lord, and Satan also
> came among them.

It is obvious Satan was in the third heaven, because that is the place where the sons of God would have presented themselves to the Heavenly Father. The "sons of God" mentioned in this verse are angelic creatures. They are not sons of God in the sense that we are. They are called sons of God because they are the creation of God.

The Apostle John writes in the Book of Revelation that Satan accuses us before the Father day and night. The Father is in the third heaven, so Satan obviously still has access to it. There is coming a day, however, when he will be extradited into the earth realm, and that will be the only place he will be able to operate until he is cast into the lake of fire. As John points out in Revelation 12:7-8:

> And war broke out in heaven: Michael and his
> angels fought with the dragon; and the dragon and
> his angels fought,
> but they did not prevail, nor was a place found
> for them in heaven any longer.

This event has not happened yet, but it is when Satan will be cast out of the heavenlies completely and totally, into the earth realm.

Knowing Our Enemy

In Revelation 12:9, John shows us something else about our enemy.

> So the great dragon was cast out, that serpent of old, called the Devil and Satan, who deceives the whole world; he was cast to the earth, and his angels were cast out with him.

Notice all these aliases. Satan is called the dragon, the serpent, the devil, as well as Lucifer, the king of Tyre, the deceiver, the tempter, and the thief. As I said at the beginning of this chapter, all these names, and some more we will look at shortly, can give us a thorough understanding of how Satan operates. That is of crucial importance to us for one very good reason.

We are told in 1 Timothy 6:12 to **Fight the good fight of faith.** To do this successfully, we must know our enemy. We must know not only that he exists, but also his mode of operation and how we are to view him. It is of vital importance to know these things, so we can know how he will attack us, and so we can be successful in our war against him.

Many people do not like talking about the devil. They consider talking about him the same as glorifying him, and they certainly do not want to do that. But when we discuss the devil and how he operates, we are not glorifying him. We are exposing him for who he really is. We are locating the enemy so that when he comes against us, we can adequately defend ourselves against him, and use our faith to blow him away!

Jesus gives us another of the devil's aliases in John 14:30, when He says:

> "I will no longer talk much with you, for the ruler of this world is coming, and he has nothing in Me."

Paul adds this in 2 Corinthians 4:3-4:

> But even if our gospel is veiled, it is veiled to those who are perishing,
> whose minds the god of this age has blinded, who do not believe, lest the light of the gospel of the glory of Christ, who is the image of God, should shine on them.

Paul does not say that the Heavenly Father has blinded the minds of those who do not believe. He says **the god of this age** has blinded them. The god of this age could not be the Heavenly Father, who **"so loved the world that He gave His only begotten Son, that whoever believes in Him should not perish but have everlasting life."** It must be another god, the one who is also referred to as the ruler of this age — alias the dragon, the serpent, the devil, Satan.

Paul gives us one more alias for this ruler in Ephesians 2:1-2, and reminds us of something else.

> And you He made alive, who were dead in trespasses and sins,

in which you once walked according to the
course of this world, according to the prince of the
power of the air, the spirit who now works in the sons
of disobedience.

The prince of the power of the air, Satan, is a
dethroned angel. He is a fallen, rebellious, disobedient
spirit creature. That spirit is the god of this world. He
is real, and the Bible tells us in several places how he
operates.

2 Timothy 2:26:

and that they may come to their senses and
escape the snare of the devil, having been taken captive by him to do his will.

If the devil does not exist, how could you be
trapped by him?

Acts 10:38:

"how God anointed Jesus of Nazareth with the
Holy Spirit and with power, who went about doing
good and healing all who were oppressed by the
devil...."

We can infer from this verse of scripture that sickness and disease are satanic oppression, that Satan is
the oppressor, and Jesus is the deliverer. Otherwise,
how could Jesus heal people who were oppressed by a
devil who does not exist?

Luke 13:15-16:

The Lord then answered him and said, "Hypocrite! Does not each one of you on the Sabbath loose his ox or donkey from the stall, and lead it away to water it?

"So ought not this woman, being a daughter of Abraham, whom Satan has bound — think of it — for eighteen years, be loosed from this bond on the Sabbath?"

This woman's infirmity was not caused by God, but by Satan. We can very clearly see that Satan is, unfortunately, alive and doing well on this planet. He will throw anything in your path to stop you or slow you down. That is why living in this earth-realm can sometimes be such a fight — or as Paul very aptly phrases it, a warfare.

2 Corinthians 10:3:

For though we walk in the flesh, we do not war according to the flesh.

2 Timothy 2:4:

No one engaged in warfare entangles himself with the affairs of this life, that he may please him who enlisted him as a soldier.

The terms *war* and *warfare* imply an opponent, a struggle, and a conflict. If you are a Christian, you are at war, and you have an enemy — hence the admonition in 1 Peter 5:8 to **Be sober, be vigilant; because your adversary the devil walks about like a roaring lion, seeking whom he may devour.**

Satan and his forces will devour you with sickness, fear, poverty, disease, warfare, bloodshed, accidents — anything he can. Once you become aware of who he is, and how he operates, however, and you become aware that he is already whipped and defeated, you will stop allowing him to lord it over you. He will be out of business, as far as you are concerned.

Take Your Authority

Christians need to stop blaming the Heavenly Father for their misfortunes, and go after the ones who are really guilty — the devil and his demon forces. You have authority over them. All you have to do is learn to use it, and act!

Luke 10:17-19:

> **Then the seventy returned with joy, saying, "Lord, even the demons are subject to us in Your name."**
> **And He said to them, "I saw Satan fall like lightning from heaven.**
> **"Behold, I give you the authority to trample on serpents and scorpions, and over all the power of the enemy, and nothing shall by any means hurt you."**

The word *power* in verse 19 is *dunamus*, which means "ability." *Trample* means "to walk on"; serpents and scorpions are aliases for the demon host.

What Jesus is actually saying is, "Behold, I give you authority over all the ability of the enemy, and nothing by any means shall hurt you." However, you will never get any of the personal benefit of that until you know it, believe it, and exercise your spiritual authority by taking the Word of God and exercising your faith. This includes the admonition the Apostle Paul gives us in Ephesians 6:11:

Put on the whole armor of God, that you may be able to stand against the wiles of the devil.

The responsibility for putting on this armor is ours. The verse does not say God will put it on for us. **Put on** means *you* do it. The reason you put it on is that, if you are not protected, you will be vulnerable to the attacks of the enemy, and you can go under. God does not want you to go under. If He did not want you protected, He would not have given you any armor.

Each piece of the armor is designed to protect a different facet of your being, and each facet has to be protected. God does not want us to have part of the armor on, and part of it off. He wants us to have the whole armor on. The word *armor* in this verse, in the Greek, is the word *panoplia*, and it means "the complete set" — all of it.

> Put on the whole armor of God, that you may be
> able to stand against the wiles of the devil.

The word *wiles* in the Greek means "deceits," or
"deception." Satan will try to deceive you, con you,
trick you any way he can with the circumstances of life,
so that you will take your armor off. Once you do that,
he can dominate you. It is a big temptation to be governed by the circumstances — and Satan has plenty of
circumstances he can hit you with.

This does not mean you should deny that the
circumstances exist. That in itself would be foolish.
However, you can deny Satan the right and privilege
to govern or control you through the circumstances.
Instead, focus your attention on the Word of God,
and through the Word, adjust the circumstances to fit
your needs.

Satan's Assistants

Ephesians 6:12:

> For we wrestle not against flesh and blood, but
> against principalities, against powers, against the
> rulers of the darkness of this age, against spiritual
> hosts of wickedness in the heavenly places.

Just as there are seraphim, cherubim, and
archangels in the ranks of God's angels, there are also
ranks in the demon hosts. The four basic ranks of

demons are principalities, powers (or authorities), rulers of the darkness of this age, and spiritual hosts of wickedness (wicked spirits) in the heavenly places.

The most powerful of these four classes are spiritual hosts of wickedness in the heavenly places. They could be referred to as the generals of the demon hosts. The rulers of the darkness of this age would be considered the captains, the powers, sergeants, and the principalities, privates. This whole world has been mapped out by Satan. He has detachments of these demon spirits and wicked angels stationed in and occupying different parts of the world to do different things.

You may or may not know it, but there are people who are manipulated and influenced by these evil spirits. There are sex-perversion spirits, narcotic spirits, alcohol spirits, tobacco spirits, and many others. I am not saying that everyone who smokes cigarettes is possessed by a tobacco spirit, or that everyone who drinks is possessed by an alcohol spirit, but many of these people can be influenced by such a spirit. And if that influence is not checked, there can come a time when these people are addicted to the point that they are controlled by it.

There are even religious spirits that work through religion to bring men into bondage, to keep them blinded from the truth of God's Word. That is really the goal of all these spirits — to keep people from finding out the truth of God's Word, of what Jesus did to free us from sin, and, failing that, of how to live by faith in that freedom in all aspects of our lives. That is the standing order from Satan, and they will do whatever they can, throw anything they can at you, to follow that order.

Certain spirits also occupy certain pieces of territory. That territory is "their turf," and they want to stay
there at all costs. A perfect example of this is found in
Mark 5:1-14, in the story of the Gadarene demoniac.

> Then they came to the other side of the sea, to the
> country of the Gadarenes.
> And when He had come out of the boat, immedi-
> ately there met Him out of the tombs a man with an
> unclean spirit,
> who had his dwelling among the tombs; and no
> one could bind him, not even with chains,
> because he had often been bound with shackles
> and chains. And the chains had been pulled apart by
> him, and the shackles broken in pieces; neither could
> anyone tame him.
> And always, night and day, he was in the moun-
> tains and in the tombs, crying out and cutting himself
> with stones.
> When he saw Jesus from afar, he ran and wor-
> shipped Him.
> And he cried with a loud voice and said, "What
> have I to do with You, Jesus, Son of the Most High
> God? I implore You by God that You do not torment
> me."
> For He said to him, "Come out of the man,
> unclean spirit!"
> Then He asked him, "What is your name?" And
> he answered, saying, "My name is Legion; for we are
> many."
> Also he begged Him earnestly that He would not
> send them out of the country.
> Now a large herd of swine was feeding there
> near the mountains.
> So all the demons begged Him, saying, "Send us
> to the swine, that we may enter them."

> And at once Jesus gave them permission. Then the unclean spirits went out and entered the swine (there were about two thousand); and the herd ran violently down the steep place into the sea, and drowned in the sea.
>
> So those who fed the swine fled, and they told it in the city and in the country. And they went out to see what it was that had happened.

Even pigs have enough sense not to be demon possessed. Rather than be demon possessed, they ran down the hill, and drowned in the sea.

Demons need a vehicle by which to manifest themselves in this physical world. What they desire most is to inhabit and possess a man. If they cannot do this, they will take the secondary step of possessing an animal. Failing that, they will go into a house or some other geographical location, and haunt or inhabit that. But their highest goal is to possess a man, because then they can do their greatest damage in this earth realm in trying to thwart the work of God.

Armor for Spiritual Warfare

These demons are ready at any time to throw whatever they can at us, and hinder us not just in our walk, but in our being good ambassadors of Christ to the world. For this reason, God tells us to do the following in Ephesians 6:13-17:

Therefore take up the whole armor of God, that you may be able to withstand in the evil day, and having done all, to stand.

Stand therefore, having girded your waist with truth, having put on the breastplate of righteousness,

and having shod your feet with the preparation of the gospel of peace;

above all, taking the shield of faith with which you will be able to quench all the fiery darts of the wicked one.

And take the helmet of salvation, and the sword of the Spirit, which is the word of God.

This armor is not for your physical body. Remember, you are not wrestling against flesh and blood in this warfare, but against demon spirits. Demon spirits are spiritual creatures. Your armor is spiritual because the warfare is spiritual. It is manifested in the physical world, but its origin is spiritual, and it is literally won or lost in the realm of the spirit.

A shield is made to ward off the thrust of an enemy, whether that thrust is with a spear, a sword, or some other weapon. With the shield of faith, you have the ability present with you **to quench all the fiery darts of the wicked one.**

Darts literally means "missiles." If you put out all the fiery darts of the wicked one, none of them should be able to get through to you. If they cannot get to you, you cannot be hurt. Therefore, if you are being hurt, at least some of the darts must be getting through.

I cannot emphasize this enough: You are in a warfare. The object of war is to kill your enemy, bomb him out, annihilate him. Satan will use poverty, fear, sickness, prejudice, strife, hate, and anything else he and his associates can get their hands on to do exactly that.

This is why I specialize in faith. Faith is the only thing that will quench the fiery darts of the wicked. If those darts are getting through to the point where they are hurting you, putting you out of business, rendering you inoperative, it means you do not have your shield up, and that you should get it up now.

Do not wait for the darts to start coming to get your armor on. While everything is well with you, while the sun is shining and there are no clouds in the sky, learn now how to walk in the full armor of God. Learn now to use the shield of faith. Learn now so that when the enemy comes in like a flood, you can raise a standard against him. It is too late when the bombs start exploding to try to figure out how to use your protection, or your weapon.

Ephesians 6:17:

And take the helmet of salvation, and the sword of the Spirit, which is the word of God.

If you examine this catalog of spiritual armor carefully, you will notice that all but one piece of that armor is for defensive purposes — to keep the enemy from coming after you. The one exception to this is the sword of the Spirit.

The word *Spirit* is capitalized here, which can make it appear that we are talking about the sword of the Holy Spirit. However, this armor is not for the Holy

Spirit's benefit — it is for yours. You put on the whole armor of God. The sword of the Spirit, which is the Word of God, was given to you. The Holy Spirit is the giver of the Word, but the Word is not given to Him. It is given to the family of God.

The sword is actually the sword of your recreated human spirit. It is the weapon your spirit uses against the enemy, and you are to use it to attack the enemy. Whenever the devil comes after us, we should be ready to do what Jesus did in the fourth chapter of Matthew — put that sword right between Satan's eyes, and say, "It is written ..." But you have to know what is written. You have to know your rights in Christ, and be prepared to stand on those rights no matter what, before you can say, "It is written."

Are we supposed to run down the road of life with the devil chasing after us? No! In fact, our "marching orders" from Jesus are these:

Mark 16:17-18:

"... In My name they shall cast out demons;... they will lay hands on the sick, and they will recover."

Luke 10:19:

"Behold, I give you the authority to trample on serpents and scorpions, and over all the power of the enemy, and nothing shall by any means hurt you."

Ephesians 4:27:

nor give place to the devil.

James 4:7:

Therefore submit to God. Resist the devil and he will flee from you.

The devil is not to chase you down the road of life, but rather, he is to flee from you.

Lie 2
Hell Is Only a State
of Mind

Just as the devil has perpetrated the lie that he does not exist, he has also spread the notion that there is no such place as hell, either.

Some years ago, there was an article entitled, "Whatever Happened to Hell?" in a prominent Black magazine. In this article, the writers had taken a poll of the major Black religious leaders of the time, and the consensus was that hell was a state of mind, not a place. The majority of them said that hell is right here on earth, and that people make their own heaven or hell here. They added that there was no such place as heaven, that heaven also was a state of mind.

At one time, the basic message in many churches was, "Repent, get saved, or you are going to hell!" It was the "hellfire-and-brimstone" message, and many people were scared into Christianity. Of course, getting saved is the thing to do, whether you are scared into it or not. But there was not much said in many of those sermons that was really traceable, as far as the Bible is concerned, to an accurate understanding of what hell is really all about.

23

Let me assure you, there is definitely such a place as heaven, and such a place as hell. It is not something preachers made up to scare people into getting saved.

Your Choice, Not God's

Some people get upset when you mention hell to them, and they use this argument: "Do you believe that a God of love would send His own children to a fiery, burning hell? Suppose you were a father. Would you consign your children to an eternal, burning hell?"

Rationally, you might think about it, and say, "Well, no ... absolutely not! I would not send my kids to hell."

They then say, "Well, neither will God send anyone to hell. So there could not be any such place as hell and eternal punishment, because a good God, a God of love, would never send anyone there."

That kind of thinking is all right rationally and academically, but these people missed the point.

Read this statement very, very carefully: God does not and will not send anyone to hell except the devil and his angels. That is whom hell was made for. Hell was never intended for mankind. According to the Bible, it is God's will that no man should perish, but that all should come to repentance.

However, God will let you go to hell if that is your choice. God has been doing everything He can for the last 2,000 years to keep you out of there. If you go there, it is because you chose to go by rejecting God's offer of clemency and redemption through Jesus Christ.

The Bible gives us an accurate knowledge of hell. Once you know what the Bible says about hell, it will be much easier for you to present your case to unsaved friends and relatives, rather than just trying to scare them into becoming Christians. You cannot simply tell people these days, "Don't go to hell," because the first thing they will say is, "What is hell?" If you cannot answer their question, they will more than likely shrug their shoulders and leave. However, the answer is right in the Bible, very simple, direct, and plain.

Where the Fire Is Not Quenched

It is interesting to note that the word *hell* appears 12 times in the New Testament. To show the importance of that word to the Kingdom of God and to spiritual matters, the Lord Jesus Christ uses the word Himself 11 of those 12 times.

Matthew 5:22, 29, 30:

"But I say to you that whoever is angry with his brother without a cause shall be in danger of the judgment. And whoever says to his brother, 'Raca!' shall be in danger of the council. But whoever says, 'You fool!' shall be in danger of hell fire....

"If your right eye causes you to sin, pluck it out and cast it from you; for it is more profitable for you that one of your members perish, than for your whole body to be cast into hell.

"And if your right hand causes you to sin, cut it off and cast it from you; for it is more profitable for you that one of your members perish, than for your whole body to be cast into hell."

Matthew 10:28:

"And do not fear those who kill the body but cannot kill the soul. But rather fear Him who is able to destroy both soul and body in hell."

Matthew 18:19:

"And if your eye causes you to sin, pluck it out and cast it from you. It is better for you to enter into life with one eye, rather than having two eyes, to be cast into hell fire."

Notice that in each of these scriptures where Jesus uses *hell*, He relates it to fire. He does not just say *hell*, but *hell fire*. Keep that in mind while we read a few more passages of scripture.

Matthew 23:15, 33:

"Woe to you, scribes and Pharisees, hypocrites! For you travel land and sea to win one proselyte, and when he is won, you make him twice as much a son of hell as yourselves....

"Serpents, brood of vipers! How can you escape the condemnation of hell?"

Mark 9:43:

"If your hand causes you to sin, cut it off. It is better for you to enter life maimed, rather than having two hands, to go to hell, into the fire that shall never be quenched."

This is a little different than what is said in Matthew. Jesus talked about hell and fire, but here He gives a little description of this fire. He says "... **the fire that shall never be quenched.**" In other words, it shall never go out.

Mark 9:45-48:

"And if your foot causes you to sin, cut it off. It is better for you to enter life lame, rather than having two feet, to be cast into hell, into the fire that shall never be quenched —
"where
'Their worm does not die,
And the fire is not quenched.'
And if your eye causes you to sin, pluck it out. It is better for you to enter the kingdom of God with one eye, rather than having two eyes, to be cast into hell fire —
"where
'Their worm does not die,
And the fire is not quenched.'"

Luke 12:5:

"But I will show you whom you should fear: Fear Him who, after He has killed, has power to cast into hell; yes, I say to you, fear Him!"

In these 11 instances, the Lord Jesus Christ Himself speaks of and uses the word *hell*. Notice that in the majority of these cases, He also associates fire with this idea of hell. It is not the Church saying this, and it is not me. Jesus is the one making this association.

The other instance in the New Testament where hell is used is James 3:6:

> And the tongue is a fire, a world of iniquity. The tongue is so set among our members that it defiles the whole body, and sets on fire the course of nature; and it is set on fire by hell.

In these 12 references, the original Greek word that was translated into *hell* is the word *Gehenna*. It is also spelled *Geenna*, and it refers to a place called the Valley of Hinnom, which was located just outside the walled city of Jerusalem.

The Valley of Hinnom was a place of renown not only in the days Jesus walked the earth, but also in the time of the Old Testament. Way back in the days of Israel, it was called the Valley of Tophet, and the fire worshippers, who worshiped the god Moloch, took their little children there and burned them as sacrifices to their pagan deity. Later, the valley became the city dump, and all the garbage from the city was taken there and burned.

Jesus used the Valley of Hinnom as a graphic example of what hell is like, because He knew the people He was ministering to at the time would know what He was talking about and would be able to relate to it. All their lives, they had seen smoke ascending from the perpetual flames. When they approached the refuse piles, they saw the worms and maggots crawling in the decomposed garbage and slush. So when Jesus said, **"Where their worm does not die, and the fire is not quenched,"** they could immediately grasp what He was talking about.

Another word in the New Testament you find translated as *hell* is the Greek word *Hades*. However, this word, as well as the Hebrew word *Sheol*, have both been mistranslated. These words refer to a definite place, but they do not refer to the garbage dump outside Jerusalem. They refer to the place where departed spirits go and where those spirits are tormented in fire.

You are a spirit. You do not have a spirit. You are one. You have a soul, and you live inside a physical body. As long as God is alive, you will never cease to be an animated, living, consciously thinking entity. Your body may cease to live, but your spirit, the real you, will continue to exist.

No Purgatory or Eternal Sleep

Now, it is not my intention to step on any denominational toes, and I apologize in advance for possibly doing so. However, I have to be faithful to the ministry of the Word of God, and I have to be honest. The Bible does not mention any intermediate place, such as purgatory or limbo, from which people can pray you into heaven. When you physically die, and your spirit and soul separate from your physical body, you go either to heaven or to hell, and what you do in this life, relative to accepting Jesus as your personal Savior and Lord, will determine your ultimate goal.

There is another group which believes there is no such thing as your being or having a spirit and a soul that is separate from your body. They view you as a soul, period. According to them, when you physically die, you cease to exist. Whatever goes into the grave stays there unconscious, unknowing, until the great day of judgment.

These people say when the day of judgment comes, if you did everything right during your physical life, you will come up in God's remembrance. When God remembers you and finds you acceptable, He will resurrect you, and you will come to life again. If you are not acceptable to God (and you will not know that until God decides to remember you), you will remain unconscious, with no life, forever. It will be like going to sleep and never waking up.

According to the Bible, this concept is not true. It is not even true in this group's Bible, printed by their own publishing house. That, to me, is absolutely amazing — that they could be deceived by a Bible they print themselves, and the part they are deceived about is not even in their Bible. It is something a man told them, and they believe the man more than they believe the Bible the man wrote. If they would read the Bible, they would find out the concept of "soul sleep" is not in there.

Where Hell Is

Again, hell or Hades is the place of the departed spirits and souls of those who physically die, who do not know Jesus Christ as their personal Savior and Lord. Hell is not a state of mind. It is an actual, geographical location. In Matthew 11:23, Jesus says the following:

"And you, Capernaum, who are exalted to heaven, will be brought down to Hades; for if the

mighty works which were done in you had been done
in Sodom, it would have remained until this day."

Here, Jesus uses the word *Hades*, not *Gehenna*, so
He is referring to a geographical location. Also notice
the word *down*. It describes a direction, and it is a very
important designation.

Jesus points out another important facet in
Matthew 16:18:

> "And I also say to you that you are Peter, and on
> this rock I will build My church, and the gates of
> Hades shall not prevail against it."

Jesus does not say that Hades will not prevail, but
that **"the gates of Hades will not prevail."** Remember
the word *down* and the reference to *gates of Hades*, and
read Luke 10:15:

> "And you, Capernaum, who are exalted to
> heaven, will be brought down to Hades."

In all three of these verses, Jesus uses the word
Hades. He also adds the term *brought* in this verse —
"brought down to Hades."

Another place where *Hades* is used, and where another
important designation is located, is Revelation 1:17-18:

> And when I saw Him, I fell at His feet as dead.
> But he laid His right hand on me, saying to me, "Do
> not be afraid; I am the First and the Last.

I am He who lives, and was dead, and behold, I
am alive forevermore. Amen. And I have the keys of
Hades and of Death."

Jesus said, **"I have the keys of Hades...."** What
would you need a key for? For the gates of Hades we
just read about in Matthew 16:18. The reason you need
gates is to secure a wall, and the reason you need a wall
is to either keep people in or to keep them out. Keys,
gates, and walls are all important designations,
because they all denote an actual place!

Jesus Went to Hell

Jesus has the key to the gate, and the word *keys*
means "authority." Jesus has that authority because of
what He did to reconcile us to God.

When Jesus died on the cross, His spirit and soul
went to hell. In three days and nights, He served the sen-
tence that we should have served throughout eternity.
After three days and nights, God said, "It is enough! Let
My Son go!" Jesus took captivity captive, His spirit and
soul came back into the earth-realm, and He walked out
of the garden tomb with a newly resurrected body.

Someone may think at this point, "That is heresy,
Brother Price! Jesus in hell?! Come on!" But wait a
minute. This is what the Bible says, not Fred Price. In
fact, let me show you what Jesus Himself said about
the subject in Matthew 12:38-40:

> Then some of the scribes and Pharisees answered, saying, "Teacher, we want to see a sign from You."
>
> But He answered and said to them, "An evil and adulterous generation seeks after a sign, and no sign will be given to it except the sign of the prophet Jonah.
>
> For as Jonah was three days and three nights in the belly of the great fish, so will the Son of Man be three days and three nights in the heart of the earth."

"In the heart of the earth." The earth is a very large piece of property — about 25,000 miles around at the equator — and if you went in a straight line through the middle of the earth from the North Pole to the South Pole, you would be traveling for at least several days. For that reason, you would not call the garden tomb the heart of anything. It was merely a hole in the side of a hill, and a few steps down into the tomb is where you would put the body.

Also, when you leave the realm of spiritual matters and look at the natural side of things, it is interesting to note that geologists tell us the closer you get to the center of the earth, the hotter it gets. They then tell us the earth is 50 million years old, and that it is still cooling. How long do you think it would take for the earth to cool down? After 50 million years, you would figure anything would be cool.

Since the days scientists began measuring the core of the earth up to the present time, they say there has been no diminishing of the heat factor. It is just as hot today as it was when they started measuring. That tells me the earth is not cooling. Considering the scriptures we have read so far, isn't that coincidental?

Let me show you a couple of more scriptures to prove this is where Jesus went, since the Bible says, "In the mouth of two or three witnesses shall every word be established."

Ephesians 4:9-10:

(Now this, "He ascended" — what does it mean but that He also first descended into the lower parts of the earth?
He who descended is also the One who ascended far above all the heavens, that He might fill [or fulfill] all things.)

Notice, **He also first descended into the lower parts of the earth.** When Jesus physically died, His spirit and soul were released from His body, and He went down into the heart, the very core of the earth, into hell itself. For three days and nights, Jesus suffered the punishment you and I should have suffered throughout eternity.

Of course, that is not the end of the story, as the Apostle Peter points out in Acts 2:27:

"'For You will not leave my soul in Hades, Nor will You allow Your Holy One to see corruption.'"

This was why Jesus was raised immediately after the third day. In the part of the world where Jesus lived, a dead body begins to decompose on the fourth day. That was the reason Martha told Jesus they did not want to roll away the stone that sealed Lazarus' tomb.

She told Him, **"Lord, by this time there is a stench, for he has been dead four days"** (John 11:39). But the Bible says prophetically that Jesus' body would never see corruption, so He was raised immediately after the third day.

Acts 2:31:

> "he, foreseeing this, spoke concerning the resurrection of the Christ, that His soul was not left in Hades, nor did His flesh see corruption."

Jesus' soul was not left in hell. He rose triumphant and became the first man to be born again. When He did that, He opened the door for all men to become sons of God and to escape the punishment of hell. But the only way someone gets the benefits of what Jesus did is to accept Him as personal Savior and Lord. If you reject Him, you have to go into hell and pay the price for yourself.

And in Hell ...

Luke 16:19-31:

> "There was a certain rich man who was clothed in purple and fine linen and fared sumptuously every day.
> "But there was a certain beggar named Lazarus, full of sores, who was laid at his gate,
> "desiring to be fed with the crumbs which fell from the rich man's table. Moreover the dogs came and licked his sores.

"So it was that the beggar died, and was carried by the angels to Abraham's bosom. The rich man also died and was buried.

"And being in torments in Hades, he lifted up his eyes and saw Abraham afar off, and Lazarus in his bosom.

"Then he cried and said, 'Father Abraham, have mercy on me, and send Lazarus that he may dip the tip of his finger in water and cool my tongue; for I am tormented in this flame.'

"But Abraham said, 'Son, remember that in your lifetime you received your good things, and Lazarus likewise evil things; but now he is comforted and you are tormented.

'And besides all this, between us and you there is a great gulf fixed, so that those who want to pass from here to you cannot, nor can those from there pass to us.'

"Then he said, 'I beg you therefore, father, that you would send him to my father's house,

"for I have five brothers, that he may testify to them, lest they also come to this place of torment.'

"Abraham said to him, 'They have Moses and the prophets; let them hear them.'

"And he said, 'No, father Abraham; but if one goes to them from the dead, they will repent.'

"But he said to him, 'If they do not hear Moses and the prophets, neither will they be persuaded though one rise from the dead.'"

Notice something important in verse 23: **"And being in torments in Hades, he lifted up his eyes...."** You cannot be tormented if you are not alive and conscious. There must have been some consciousness in that place, because the rich man could see and he could feel.

Some people say, "Well, yes, Brother Price, but, of course, you realize this is just a parable."

Let me ask you this question. Was Jesus a man who changed direction in His teaching, going first one way, then another, leaving people in confusion? No. Jesus was a man who was consistent in His teaching. He would follow a course, stay on it, and would not deviate.

If this were a parable, it certainly would be unique among the many parables Jesus taught. It is so radically different from all His other parables that, if it were truly a parable, understanding why He made such a grand departure with this one story and not with any other would be mindboggling.

The departure in this story is that it is the only story Jesus taught in which He used anyone's name. In every other, He would say, "A man went out and bought a field," "A man found a pearl of great price," or something like that. However, in this story, He uses the names of Abraham and Lazarus.

Why use specific names if they were not relevant to a real-life situation? The people Jesus was telling the story to could relate to and understand the illustration or truth Jesus was trying to bring out in it, because they probably knew who Lazarus was. They may have seen him begging all the time when he was still alive. They also knew about Abraham's bosom, because that was the place of rest for those who were under the Old Covenant when they died.

I believe this story is an accurate real-life account of that place beyond the grave that everyone who does not know Jesus Christ as Savior will go to. I also believe the reason this account is in the Bible is to let us know it is one place to avoid at all costs!

If God is going to be just, He has to give us a description of heaven and a description of the place that is opposite to heaven. Otherwise, we would have no choice. If we do not know what the other place is like, we would not know whether we want to go there or go to heaven when we physically die.

We hear about the glory, the light, harmony, peace, the Tree of Life, and the Waters of Life in the City of God. We hear about all the beautiful foundations garnished with precious stones, about the gates of pearls and the streets of gold, about the Lamb who is the light thereof, and about the fact there is no night there.

But in that other place, there is torment, fire and darkness. If you do not know Jesus as your personal Savior and Lord, that is where you will go when you die.

I am not trying to scare you. I am trying to inform you. If you are going to hell, you should at least know what you are going to. And if you are going there, you will be living there. Hell is not even the worst place you will go to if you do not know Jesus as your personal Savior. Hell is a playground compared to the lake of fire.

Revelation 20:10:

> **The devil, who deceived them, was cast into the lake of fire and brimstone where the beast and the false prophet are. And they will be tormented day and night forever and ever.**

It says they will be tormented day and night, for ever and ever.

Revelation 20:13-15:

> The sea gave up the dead who were in it, and Death and Hades delivered up the dead who were in them. And they were judged, each one according to his works.
>
> Then Death and Hades were cast into the lake of fire. This is the second death.
>
> And anyone not found written in the Book of Life was cast into the lake of fire.

Dear friend, the good news is, if you do not know Jesus Christ as your personal Lord and Savior, you can be redeemed and become a child of God. You do not have to go to hell, and God does not want you to go there, either. He sacrificed His only begotten Son so that you would not have to go there. He loves you that much. If you go to hell, it means you chose to go. If you go there, you will stay in hell, then in the lake of fire, forever, because it will be too late to change your mind.

This is not a scare tactic. This is a fact. God does not want you to become a Christian out of fear, but out of love. However, He wants to show you what will happen on both sides of the scale, so that when you make your decision, you will know that you know what you have chosen. You will not be able to get angry at someone else and say, "God, someone tricked me." No. It will be your fault.

Lie 3
You Do Not Need
to Study the Bible
If You Go to Church

Many times — especially if a person has come from a traditional religious background and is not familiar with our ministry — we have had visitors come to Crenshaw Christian Center for a Sunday worship service without a Bible. They are ready to sit like a bump on a log, sing a few songs, and be preached to before they go out to Sunday brunch. They see everyone around them pick up their Bibles just before I start teaching, watch them turn to each scripture I mention, and either "get with the program" quickly or feel like a fish out of water.

. That is not the fault of these individuals. It is an attitude that has been bred into many people: The preacher is your spiritual guide, and the preacher is always right. He will tell you everything you need to know about living the Christian life. You do not need to know anything on your own.

This is a highly dangerous attitude, because, in most cases, the preacher may not have read the Bible himself. He may know what the denomination, the seminary, and tradition say about a particular subject, but he may not know what God has to say. The preacher is just as human as you are, which means he may give you the wrong information, because what he says and what God says can be entirely different.

Let me give you an example of what I mean. Granted, this may seem an extreme case, but it will illustrate my point. I do not say this to denigrate this person, but to use him as an example of what I am talking about and the tragic results which can result from it. Also, since what happened to this person and the people in his ministry took place a number of years ago, it has become something of public record.

"Get My Teaching"

Just after I came into the knowledge of the Word, and started learning what the Bible said about how God can work supernaturally in our lives, one of the people at the church I pastored told me about the Reverend Jim Jones. This person said that great spiritual and supernatural things were happening in this man's ministry.

I was interested in anything that was supernatural in terms of the things of God, and I wanted to be right there when God was operating supernaturally in order to learn everything I could. This person told me that Jones was having some meetings in the Los Angeles area, so I went with a friend of mine to see what was going on.

By the time we got to the auditorium where the meeting was being held, the place was packed, and we got two seats in the last row of the auditorium. The place was literally rocking, as the congregation had been singing for quite some time. All of a sudden, a lady in the front row jumped out of her seat and said, "Praise the Lord, praise the Lord, thank you Jesus, thank you Jesus, thank you Jesus, thank you Jesus."

Jones had been sitting on the platform all this time, quiet, with a pair of dark sunglasses on. When he heard this lady, he came to the pulpit. He stared down at her, and with a stern voice, he said, "We will have none of that here! You have to get my teaching."

When I heard Jones say this, my first thought was, "You mean we cannot praise the Lord here? We cannot say, 'Thank you, Jesus'?"

Later, when he got into his message, Jones told the congregation, "You do not need this Bible. You have to get my teaching. Even Jesus said, when He sent His disciples out, 'Carry no *script* with you,' and *script* is short for Scripture. You do not need this Book!"

We got out of that place very quickly. To show you that you definitely need "this Book," a few years later, Jones convinced hundreds of his followers to quit their jobs, sell their houses, and follow him to the jungles of Guyana in South America. Eventually, he ordered them all to take communion with poisoned Kool-Aid, and had them all commit suicide.

Check It Out With the Word

The Apostle John warns us in 1 John 4:1, **Beloved, do not believe every spirit, but test the spirits, whether they are of God; because many false prophets have gone out into the world.** In order to test the spirits, we need something as a guide to test them with. That guide is the Word of God. If you remove the Bible, you have nothing to measure by.

There is no way the Holy Spirit will say, "You do not need this Book." He gives us only things based on the Word of God, and everything God tells the Holy Spirit to give us is based directly on the Bible. There is no doubt that God uses men to proclaim the Gospel, but you have to test the spirit that is behind what the man is saying. The only way you will know if what he is saying is valid is by the Word of God.

Even when you cannot initially understand what someone is saying or teaching, the basis for your accepting or rejecting it should be the Word of God. The Holy Spirit should witness to you as to whether or not what a minister is saying is right. The Word will act as a bridge for that revelation. In fact, I constantly encourage people to check out what I am saying by checking the Word for themselves. That way, they will know that they know what the Bible says about what I am talking about.

The bottom line is, the devil wants you to stay ignorant. He does not want you to learn what God has available for you through Jesus Christ. He does not want you to know what rights are yours, or that through Christ you have the victory over him in all areas of your life. Satan wants you one way — whipped, defeated and ignorant — so he can keep messing your life up every chance he gets.

The only way you will get out of that rut is by studying the Word for yourself. Yes, you should go to a church where they meet your spiritual needs. Yes, you should go to Bible study. Yes, it is a good idea to listen to cassette tapes and watch TV programs where they teach the uncompromising Word. However — and this is a big however — if you do not check out what they are saying with the Word, and continue to build on that foundation by studying the Word on your own, you will get very little real benefit out of it.

Notice what the Holy Spirit says through the Apostle Paul in 2 Timothy 2:15:

> Be diligent to present yourself approved to God, a worker who does not need to be ashamed, rightly dividing the word of truth.

The fact this verse says **rightly dividing** indicates you can wrongly divide if you do not study. The only reason you use rightly is to distinguish from wrongly.

We are told, in effect, to be diligent. The original King James Bible puts it even more bluntly, telling us, **Study to shew thyself approved unto God.** Very few people take the time and effort to study. They do not realize there is a difference between reading and studying. When you study something, you go over it again and again, until it is virtually a part of you.

God has fully revealed Himself and made Himself fully available to us through His Word. It is an encyclopedia of facts, a history book on the subject of Christianity, and a biography of Himself. Therefore, to study God's Word is to be in touch with God Himself, because God is in His Word.

You should study, first of all, to please God rather than people. Second, you should realize that you, as a Believer, need to have a workman's equipment to do your work — and you are a worker, not a vacationer, nor someone on strike or on sabbatical.

By studying the Word of God, you become equipped with the knowledge of God — knowledge which is imperative to your living the victorious Christian life. Second Timothy says we should each be **a workman who does not need to be ashamed.** That implies there are workmen who are already ashamed, who are whipped and defeated in life, but who do not need to be that way.

If you study the Word and apply it to your life, you will not be ashamed. The enemy is going to put some pressures on your life with the express purpose of shaming you, wrecking your testimony, and keeping you in defeat. But once you make the Word a part of you through study, you do not have to put up with his antics.

A Statement of Truth, or Just Truly Stated?

Another interesting point is stated for us in 2 Timothy 3:16-17:

All Scripture is given by inspiration of God, and is profitable for doctrine, for reproof, for correction, for instruction in righteousness, that the man of God may be complete, thoroughly equipped for every good work.

The fact that all scripture is profitable for instruction in righteousness ties in directly with 2 Timothy 2:15. If you do not take instruction in righteousness, how can you live the life of righteousness that God expects you to live? How can you expect to become *complete* or mature in the things of God if you never learn about spiritual matters?

Notice something else here. Paul says that all scripture — the whole Word of God — *is given by inspiration* of God. It does not say all scripture is inspired. There is a very important difference in those two terms.

In other words, everything in the Bible is not a statement of truth. However, everything in the Bible is truly stated.

Before you jump to conclusions, let me give you an illustration to prove my point. Let us say you are a stockholder at the annual meeting of the XYZ Corporation, and I am the president of the company. During the meeting, I make the statement, "All dogs come into this world with two heads and three tails."

The secretary takes all this down, and the next year we have another stockholders' meeting. As president, I call the meeting to order, and ask the secretary to read the minutes of the last meeting. When she gets to a certain point in the minutes, she says, "... and President Price said that all dogs come into this world with two heads and three tails."

What I said in the meeting is not a statement of truth. Dogs are not born with two heads and three tails. However, what I said was truly stated, because I said it in the meeting and the secretary recorded it.

If you do not know the difference between what is truly stated and a statement of truth, and how to rightly divide one from the other, you may take something that is truly stated out of the Bible and try to apply it to your life as though it were a statement of truth. Satan will take the very thing you took out of the Bible, wrap it around your neck, and use it to kill you and destroy everything you have. God will not be in a position to do anything about it, and you will think you are doing right.

The fact that many people use what happened in the Book of Job typifies what I mean. In the first chapter of Job, the devil brought all sorts of challenges against Job. He stole all of Job's cattle, his sheep, all the man had from a material standpoint. Then he killed Job's children. After all this happened, the Bible says the following:

Job 1:20-21:

Then Job arose, tore his robe, and shaved his head; and he fell to the ground and worshiped. And he said:

"Naked I came from my mother's womb,
And naked shall I return there.
The Lord gave, and the Lord has taken away;
Blessed be the name of the Lord."

Thank God for the faithfulness of Job. Thank God that when his world literally came apart, he could keep his composure and worship the Lord, instead of going to pieces. That says something about the man and his commitment to

48

the Lord. However, what Job said is not a statement of truth. It is truly stated, because it is recorded in the Bible, but it should not be construed as a statement of truth.

God did not take anything away from Job, just as He does not take anything from His children today, because the Bible says that all the gifts of God are without repentance. In other words, they are irrevocable (Rom. 11:29). Satan took everything from Job, and he is still stealing from Christians who do not know any better. They listen to preachers who do not rightly divide the Word of God say, "The Lord has given, and the Lord has taken away; blessed be the name of the Lord." Instead of checking things out for themselves, they figure, "You cannot fight God," and consider the subject closed.

That is a mistake!

You may say, "But God permitted the devil to do all that to Job." That is right. What you may fail to realize is that God had to permit it. He gave Job, and each of us, a free will. Permitting all those things to happen was Job's decision. If Job allowed it, God had to permit it.

In fact, Job brought what happened to him on himself. He says in Job 3:25, **"For the thing I greatly feared has come upon me, and what I dreaded has happened to me."** Proverbs 18:21 tells us, **Death and life are in the power of the tongue, and those who love it will eat its fruit.** That is a spiritual law. Because Job kept running off at the mouth about how scared he was, what he was afraid of came to pass.

We have a free will, and we are the instruments of God in terms of His Word. If we do not know how to use these tools, or how to use the right tools, we will be victimized. There is such a thing as learning the wrong lesson from a situation. We need to be very careful that we learn the right lesson when we study the Word of God, not the wrong one.

"And Searched the Scriptures Daily"

Acts 17:11:

These were more fair-minded than those in Thessalonica, in that they received the word with all readiness, and searched the Scriptures daily to find out whether these things were so.

I cannot stress this too strongly. It is your responsibility to search the scriptures. Going to some church or Bible study group that teaches the Bible verse by verse and chapter by chapter does not exonerate you from searching the scriptures for yourself.

The reason we need to study the scriptures daily is shown to us very clearly in the fourth chapter of Matthew.

Matthew 4:1-3:

Then Jesus was led up by the Spirit into the wilderness to be tempted by the devil.

And when He had fasted forty days and forty nights, afterward He was hungry.

Now when the tempter came to Him, he said, "If You are the Son of God, command that these stones become bread."

The devil used the same line with Adam in the garden of Eden. "Has God indeed said?..." The devil's primary objective is to get you to question God's Word. The moment you do that, you enter into the realm of doubt and unbelief, and you are completely vulnerable.

The easiest way to keep from getting messed up is to do what the Word says. The reason God tells you what to do in His Word is not to run your life for you, but to keep you from getting into trouble. I am sure you will agree it is much easier by far to stay out of a bad situation than it is to get out of a bad situation once you are in it. Notice, Jesus shows us in the next verse how to stay out of a bad situation.

Matthew 4:4:

> But He answered and said, "It is written, 'Man shall not live by bread alone, but by every word that proceeds from the mouth of God.'"

You stay out of a bad situation by learning the Word, living the Word, and standing on the Word when Satan brings the floods of life against you. Now notice something extremely important in the next couple of verses.

Matthew 4:5-6:

> Then the devil took Him up into the holy city, set Him on the pinnacle of the temple, and said to Him, "If you are the Son of God, throw Yourself down. For it is written:
> 'He shall give His angels charge over you,' and,
> 'In their hands they shall bear you up,
> Lest you dash your foot against a stone.'"

Here is the devil quoting scripture. That is why God tells us, **Be diligent to present yourself approved to God, a worker who does not need to be ashamed.** That is why He tells us to study the scriptures daily.

You have an enemy who knows and quotes the Bible. He does not understand the revelation of the Word of God, but he knows chapters and verses — and he is counting on your not knowing them. The devil will try to slip something by you that sounds so close to the truth that he hopes you will not be able to tell the difference. You had better know the Word, so you can do what Jesus did in the next verse when the enemy tries that strategy on you:

Matthew 4:7:

> Jesus said to him, "It is written again, 'You shall not tempt the Lord your God.'"

Have the Sword of the Spirit Ready

The devil came to Jesus three times in the fourth chapter of Matthew. Each time, Jesus parried the thrust of the devil by saying, "It is written," then quoting what was written, and the devil could not deal with it.

The devil cannot deal with the Word. He will deal with your human speculation. When you start saying, "Well, I think," the devil will whip you every way but loose. That is why God tells you to put on the armor of God and does not ever tell you to take it off. He tells us through Paul in Ephesians 6:13-17:

> Therefore take up the whole armor of God, that you may be able to withstand in the evil day, and having done all, to stand.
>
> Stand therefore, having girded your waist with truth, having put on the breastplate of righteousness,
>
> and having shod your feet with the preparation of the gospel of peace;
>
> above all, taking the shield of faith with which you will be able to quench all the fiery darts of the wicked one.
>
> And take the helmet of salvation, and the sword of the Spirit, which is the word of God.

If you look carefully at this list, you will notice that all but one piece of the armor is for defensive purposes. The only piece to be used for offensive purposes is the sword of the Spirit — the Word of God. We also have the name of Jesus, but the name of Jesus works in line with the Word, not in place of it.

In other words, the Word of God is the only weapon you have. You do not walk around saying, "In Jesus' name. In Jesus' name. In Jesus' name." You have to say something in Jesus' name. When you stand on the Word of God and make a declaration based on what is written in the Word in Jesus' name, it carries power. And you are supposed to use that power whenever the enemy tries to attack you.

Hosea 4:6 tells us:

> My people are destroyed for lack of knowledge....

This verse does not say, "My people are destroyed because they do not go to church," or, "My people are

53

destroyed because they do not pay their tithes." It says, **My people are destroyed for lack of knowledge —** knowledge about God, His way, and His will — because they do not take the time to get the knowledge from His Word! They are not taking the time to learn how to use their weapon, and they are getting cut down in droves.

Ephesians 6:12:

> For we do not wrestle against flesh and blood, but against principalities, against powers, against the rulers of the darkness of this age, against spiritual hosts of wickedness in the heavenly places.

We do have an enemy, but he is a spiritual enemy, not a flesh-and-blood enemy. Our warfare is a spiritual warfare, which is why Paul tells us to **take ... the sword of the Spirit, which is the word of God.** This warfare manifests in the physical realm, in sickness, disease, and other challenges, but the real root of the warfare is spiritual.

The more you can get the Word into you, the more that Word can come out of your mouth, and the more you can stand against the issues of life this warfare brings against you. As Jesus points out in Mark 11:23:

> "For assuredly, I say to you, whoever SAYS to this mountain, 'Be removed and be cast into the sea,' and does not doubt in his heart, but believes that those things he SAYS will be done, he shall have whatever he SAYS."

It is vitally important for you to know the Word is real and to have confidence that it is the Word of God. If you do not have that confidence, you will not say it, and if you do not say it, it will never work for you.

Paul adds this in Romans 10:17:

> **So then faith comes by hearing, and hearing by the word of God.**

Notice, this verse does not say who you have to hear the Word from. You can hear it from yourself. The more you hear it, the more it will build up your faith. And the more your faith is built up, the more likely it is for whatever you say to come to pass. That is a spiritual law.

Finally, Paul tells us in 1 Timothy 6:12:

> **Fight the good fight of faith....**

That is the fight we are constantly in. It is true that as far as personalities are involved, Satan and his demons are the enemy, but it is our faith that is up for grabs. That is what the devil is after, and that is all he is interested in, because he knows if he can separate us from our faith, he can defeat us. If we can keep our faith up — by building it up with the Word of God and by using it — we will defeat him.

Do you see how this cycle works? The Word — Faith — Victory. Without the Word, you will not have faith, and if you do not have faith, you will not have victory in your life. That is why the Church, by and large, has been whipped and defeated for most of the past 2,000 years — because the devil has cleverly kept the Word out of the average church.

Get the Word into you. Hear the Word all day long. Constantly exposing yourself to it is what will get it into your spirit. That is why the Bible says, **So then faith comes by hearing** — and hearing, and hearing, and hearing, and hearing. It is something you must do continually.

Remember the parable of the sower? How as soon as the seed was planted, the fowls of the air would swoop down to devour it? Satan continually tries to do just that. As soon as the seed of the Word is planted, Satan is trying to pluck it up — by discouraging you, by harassing you, and by whatever means he can think of. We therefore have to continue driving the Word into our spirits until it germinates and takes root, so we can receive and hold onto the truth of the Word of God.

God wants you to win against the enemy, and He has given you everything you need to do so. That is why He calls it **the good fight of faith** — because you have every opportunity to lord that victory over the devil. That is, provided you do your part. That includes building up your faith, using it, and studying the Word of God to show yourself approved, rightly dividing the Word of truth.

These are the things you must do on an every-day, every-hour, every-minute basis. It is a lifestyle. Once you start doing these things regularly, and start living by faith as the Bible tells us to, you will see the difference between victory and defeat become increasingly apparent in your life.

Lie 4
If God Did Not Want Me
to Sin,
I Would Not Feel Like
Doing It

When we were born again, we were legally set free from sin. Sin has no legal dominion over us, and we do not have to give into it when temptation comes. Instead, we can say, "No, I refuse to do that, praise God. I've been set free from sin by Christ Jesus. Praise you for the victory, Lord, in Jesus' name."

Many Christians do not stand in this victory, or if they do stand, they do not do so for very long. Many of them have this attitude: "Well, I'm just doing what comes naturally. If God did not want me to do it, I would not feel like doing it."

That is a lie from the devil. If you believed that statement and sinned because you believed it, you did not resist the sin. Satan put that thought in your mind to bring you into bondage!

You need to see yourself as God sees you — not as Satan sees you, and not as other men see you, but as God says He sees you in His Word. Until you learn to do this, you will continue to be whipped, defeated, in bondage, and you will not live a life at the level of your privileges in Christ.

The New Creature — You

The Apostle Paul tells us in 2 Corinthians 5:17:

> **Therefore, if anyone is in Christ, he is a new creation; old things have passed away; behold, all things have become new.**

The original King James Bible says you are a "new creature." Another translation says you are a new "species."

However, when Paul says, **... old things have passed away; behold, all things have become new,** you must understand, **all things** refer to all things in the spirit realm, not all things in the natural. If what is said in this verse applied to all things in the natural, if you had a bald head the day before you got saved, you would have a head full of hair the day after you got saved. If you had no teeth, false teeth, or freckles on your nose the day before you accepted Jesus, you would not have those things the day after you accepted Him. This does not happen, however.

In other words, your physical appearance does not become new the day after you are saved. You become a new creation in the spirit, the inner man, and you should let your spirit and the Word of God take charge of your body, instead of your body taking charge of your spirit. Your body will do anything and everything you let it do until you understand the fact that your body cannot be trusted, that it has not changed — and will not change until Jesus comes back — and that you have to do something about your body.

There was a song many years ago that went, "I looked at my hands, and they looked new. I looked at my feet, and they did, too." People tended, and some still tend, to equate the new birth with an outward change. It was, perhaps, because they did not really know how to explain or understand the Bible, but because they did not really understand the import of what they were saying, the statements they made were very misleading.

These people were trying to say that a change *had* occurred. They were right — a change had occurred — and they were trying to understand what had taken place. Because they saw some alterations in physical habits — people who had stopped drinking, cursing, smoking cigarettes, chasing women or chasing men — they equated what had happened completely to outward things.

There should be some outward changes. As children of God, we should talk, think and act differently than we did before we got saved. However, it should be based on the fact that our natures have changed, not as an outward, perfunctory performance.

An outward change by itself can be forced, and it can be done by an unsaved person as easily as by a Christian. Just have the man's doctor tell him, "Stop doing this or you will die," and unless the man has a death wish, he will change his ways quickly. However, for the Christian, the outward change should be the natural outcome of the change that has occurred on the inside.

Again, that does not mean we do not have to keep an eye on our bodies. You have to watch your flesh. You cannot trust it. Even the Apostle Paul had to keep an eye on his body, even though the Spirit of God worked mightily through him. He writes in 1 Corinthians 9:27:

> But I discipline my body and bring it into subjection, lest, when I have preached to others, I myself should become disqualified.

In the original King James Bible, Paul says, **But I keep under my body....** I like that, because it lets me know that it is a continuous act, which most definitely takes discipline.

Discipline takes time and effort. It takes work. It is an every-day, every-hour, every-minute, every-second job — and if a mighty man of God such as Paul had to do it, you do, too.

Paul covers disciplining our bodies in greater detail in the sixth chapter of Romans. In verse six, he writes:

> knowing this, that our old man was crucified with Him [Christ], that the body of sin might be done away with, that we should no longer be slaves of sin.

Notice, **...that we should no longer be slaves of sin.** It does not say that we *would* no longer be slaves of sin. It says we *should* no longer be its slaves. That means being enslaved by sin is our choice.

60

Unfortunately, the translators lost some of the meaning and impact of what the Spirit of God was saying here. The word translated here as *sin* in the Greek should literally be *sinful nature*. A sinner is a sinner because of his nature, not because of an isolated act of sin such as lying or stealing. That is why Jesus says in John 3:7, **"You must be born again."** The only way you can change the old nature is by getting a new one, and the way you get a new one is by the new birth.

The phrase *done away with* also does not convey its true meaning in the original language. Usually, when we think of something that is done away with (at least in the English language), we think of it as though it no longer exists. However, in the Greek, *done away with* means "rendered inactive." The thing may still exist, but it does not have any control or authority over you.

Keeping this in mind, we can read Romans 6:6 this way:

> knowing this, that our old man was crucified with Him, that the body of the sinful nature might be rendered inactive, that we should no longer be slaves of sin.

Notice also that Paul does not say that the sinful nature was rendered inactive. He says that it *might* be. We still have the opportunity to serve sin after we are born again, but we do not have to rush in and take advantage of the opportunity to sin.

Romans 6:7:

> For he who has died has been freed from sin.

61

The word *died*, like *done away with*, is misleading. A more literal translation would be *justified* or *declared righteous*. This verse should read, "For he who has been justified, or declared righteous, has been freed from sin." Again, it does not mean sin is not there. It means we do not have to have anything to do with sin any more.

Romans 6:11:

> **Likewise you also, reckon yourselves to be dead indeed to sin** [here, again, it should be the sinful nature], **but alive to God in Christ Jesus our Lord.**

The word *reckon* means "to treat as though," or "to count as." In other words, **reckon ... to be dead** means "to act like your body is dead."

Romans 6:12:

> **Therefore do not let sin** [here the word should be sin] **reign in your mortal body, that you should obey it in its lusts.**

God tells you, **Do not let sin reign.** That means you cannot cop out with excuses like, "I couldn't help myself." You could help yourself, because God told you not to let sin reign, and He would not tell you to do anything you could not do. If you say, "I couldn't help myself," you are lying.

Romans 6:13:

And do not present your members as instruments of unrighteousness to sin [the word sin here
should be the sinful nature], but present yourselves to
God as being alive from the dead, and your members
as instruments of righteousness to God.

The sinful nature can work only through the members that are available to it. If no members are available
to it, it cannot do anything. Righteous instruments do
not steal cookies out of the cookie jars of life. They do not
commit fornication or adultery. They do not tell lies, gossip, envy, or operate in strife. The reason why they do
not do these things is spelled out in the next verse.

Romans 6:14:

For sin [the sinful nature] shall not have dominion
over you, for you are not under law but under grace.

If we read verse 14 first, and follow it with verse
11, you will notice something very dramatic:

For the sinful nature shall not have dominion
over you....
[if you] reckon yourselves to be dead to the sinful nature.

Counting yourself to be dead to sin is the only way
the sinful nature will not have control over you. As far as

God is concerned, that old nature has been crucified with Christ. If you really think about your body being dead to sin, you will find out how easy it can be to live righteously.

This is why the Bible tells us to consider ourselves dead to sin, and this is where faith comes in. There will be times when your body will not feel dead. In fact, sometimes you may feel so alive that you think you are going to die if you do not do something about it. That is when you have to stand by faith on God's Word. Otherwise, you will mess up.

Your Body — A Holy Sacrifice

The reason God wants us to consider ourselves dead to sin is spelled out in Romans 12:1:

> **I beseech you therefore, brethren, by the mercies of God, that you present your bodies a living sacrifice, holy, acceptable to God, which is your reasonable service.**

God wants you to be holy, and He says here that it is your *reasonable* service. That means you can do it, if you are so inclined. Even if you want to say, "I don't know if I can quit smoking," or drinking, or whatever, remember, **... He who is in you is greater than he who is in the world.** If you say, "I can't do it," you are saying that Satan is stronger than God. Are you ready for that?

The question really is, "Do you *want* to be holy?" You can be holy. If anyone should know about holiness, it is God and Jesus. After all, God created you, and Jesus redeemed you and bought you with His own blood.

The next question then becomes, *"Will* you be holy?" That is the issue at hand, and it is your choice. No one will twist your arm to be holy, as far as God is concerned, but the fact God says to be holy means you can do it.

God's plan is that, through the Word, we continually train and feed our spirits, so our spirits will take control of our souls, and our souls will take control of our bodies. That is a full-time job.

We are also told to make our bodies **acceptable to God** — not to tradition, not to the denomination, but to God. You may be very acceptable to a particular denomination, the deacon board, or the people who see you in church every Sunday, but if you do not pass God's inspection, forget it.

God will hold you accountable for what you do with your body until Jesus returns. If you want to keep abusing your body with liquor, drugs, or cancer sticks (cigarettes), or keep chasing every man or woman you think you cannot live without, go ahead — that is, if you think you can get away with it when you answer to God for it. The first thing God will tell you about is, "My Word says you can do all things through Christ, Who strengthens you, so why did you really mess up?"

Romans 12:2:

> And do not be conformed to this world, but be transformed by the renewing of your mind, that you may prove what is that good and acceptable and perfect will of God.

Conformed to this world means "to be shaped like the world is shaped." Do not do something just because the world does it. Do not tell the same dirty jokes everyone else in the office tells, or use the same foul language. Be different. If you cannot be different, shut your mouth and keep it shut.

The next thing Paul says in Romans 12:2 is, **But be transformed.** How are you transformed? **By the renewing of your mind....**

As I said before, the only part of you that is born again is your spirit. You have the same mind, the same emotions, and the same body you had before you were saved, and you will have them until Jesus returns. Besides, you cannot renew something unless it is already there. If you did become transformed by receiving a new mind, instead of renewing the old one, then this verse would say, "... but be ye transformed by receiving a new mind." But this verse does not say that. It says, **... renew.**

The way you renew your mind is to feed it on the Word of God. When you want to put a new program into a computer, you have to put some information into it. You can do the same thing to your mind with the Word of God.

When pressure comes, whatever you have "programmed" into you is what will come out of your mouth, because the Word says, **... out of the abundance of the heart the mouth speaks.** When you constantly renew your mind with the Word of God, the Word will come out of your mouth, and it will go into action on the circumstances of life to work on your behalf.

When you renew your mind with the Word of God, you will know what is good, acceptable and perfect with God. The Word of God reveals the will of God, and what is acceptable to Him. Not only that, but Paul says in Romans 12:2 that we can prove this. There are only two places in the Bible in which God challenges men to prove Him. One has to do with tithing, and the other has to do with renewing your mind.

Once you renew your mind, the Word will begin to control and direct your physical body. When your body is directed in line with God's Word, you will be in the will of God. You will be out of the will of Satan, and you will be out of trouble.

Part of what should happen when your body is directed in line with God's Word is stated in Ephesians 4:17-24:

> This I say, therefore, and testify in the Lord, that you should no longer walk as the rest of the Gentiles walk, in the futility of their mind,
>
> having their understanding darkened, being alienated from the life of God, because of the ignorance that is in them, because of the blindness of their heart [or spirit];
>
> who, being past feeling, have given themselves over to lewdness, to work all uncleanness with greediness.
>
> But you have not so learned Christ,
>
> if indeed you have heard Him and have been taught by Him, as the truth is in Jesus:
>
> that you put off, concerning your former conduct....

The word *conduct*, according to the original Greek, includes your total lifestyle — what you say and how you act. Everything we say and do constitutes our conduct.

67

> ... that you put off, concerning your former con-
> duct, the old man which grows corrupt according to
> the deceitful lusts,
> and be renewed in the spirit of your mind,
> and that you put on the new man which was created
> according to God, in true righteousness and holiness.

What Paul is saying here, in essence, is this. Your spirit-man, the real you, which is on the inside, has been made a new creature in Christ Jesus. However, that man on the inside cannot be seen from the outside unless you put him on the outside and cover up "the old man" with him. What is on the outside? Your physical body. If you take the Jesus in your spirit and put Him on the outside by making your body act like Jesus would act, then people will be able to see what is on the inside.

Seek Things Which Are Above

One very important thing we should do when we "put on the new man" is stated in Colossians 3:1:

> If then you were raised with Christ, seek those
> things which are above, where Christ is, sitting at the
> right hand of God.

Many Christians are hung up on seeking the things of the earth to the utter exclusion of the things which are above. Do not get me wrong. The things of this earth which are good, which are right, which pro- mote life, are for Christians, and the Bible tells us that

God will meet our needs in abundance, according to His riches in glory by Christ Jesus. However, you have to keep your priorities straight.

Jesus says in Matthew 6:33, **"But seek FIRST the kingdom of God and His righteousness, and all these things shall be added to you."** When you get the kingdom first, then and only then will you be in a position to handle everything else without having those things hang you up. Jesus is not telling us not to have things. He is telling you to get everything in the right order so the things will not have you.

Having everything you want without seeking the kingdom first will not necessarily make you happy. Many times, the people who are financially and materially well-off are the ones who are personally, deep down, very unhappy. They are miserable because the main part of their life — the spiritual part — is missing, even though they have all of what we may think makes life worth living.

God wants you to get the spiritual part of your life together first, because only then do you have the capacity to appreciate and enjoy the rest — and God wants you to have the rest. He is the One who created it, and He created it for us.

When we read Romans 12:2, I mentioned that we should not be conformed to this world, but transformed by the renewing of our minds. This is also stated in Colossians 3:2, which says:

> **Set your mind on things above, not on things on the earth.**

To set something means "to pick out a spot, set it there, and leave it there." The way you set your mind on things above is by setting it on the Word, by continually talking about and repeating the Word.

The Word of God is the book about "above," and it will tell you how to set your mind. The beautiful part is, when you set your mind on the Word and apply the Word to your life, it will make your life work as it should. It will allow you to operate in this environment with power that can overcome every obstacle you will be challenged with.

Learning to be an overcomer is another reason Satan has very cleverly kept the Bible out of many churches. If he can keep the Bible out of you and you out of the Bible, you will not learn how to set your mind. You will end up setting your mind strictly on the things of the earth — and getting thoroughly messed up in the process.

Put Off All These

We have already talked about putting off adultery, fornication, and other things we would obviously call sins. However, these sins are not the only things God tells us to stop doing. Paul says in Colossians 3:8:

> But now you yourselves are to put off all these: anger, wrath, malice, blasphemy, filthy language out of your mouth.

These things must also be inconsistent with living a godly life and with keeping our minds renewed by the Word. Otherwise, God would not tell us to stop doing them. Also, if God tells us to put off things like anger, for instance, then we must be able to put them off, so we really have no excuse for not doing it.

"But Brother Price, it cannot be done that easy, can it?"

Yes, thank God, it is just that easy. The enemy will use things like anger to keep you off-balance and to nullify your testimony to others. But when you use your faith to put sin off, you will find that you are in control. There are plenty of things that would upset me if I let them, but I do not let them. I say, "Praise the Lord. I cast that care on the Lord. Lord, you stay awake and handle it. I am going to sleep."

There is such a thing as righteous indignation, but that is something entirely different from what I am talking about here. Some things should make you mad — mad enough to stop doing them. Jesus was righteously indignant when He threw the moneychangers out of the temple, but He did not do it with a smile on His face. You can rest assured of that.

Paul also instructs us in Colossians 3:8 to put off malice. Too many Christians hold things against their brothers and sisters in Christ, and some of them, I am well persuaded, go to an early grave because of it. In fact, did you know if you do not forgive someone for something he did to you, your Heavenly Father cannot forgive you for anything, either? Let me prove it to you. In Mark 11:25-26, Jesus tells us the following:

"And whenever you stand praying, if you have anything against anyone, forgive him, that your Father in heaven may also forgive you your trespasses.

71

"But if you do not forgive, neither will your Father in heaven forgive your trespasses."

That is an awesome thought. God will not forgive you not because He is being cruel, but because that is how He has designed the system. We have had the love of God shed abroad in our hearts. Therefore, since God forgives us for all our mistakes and mess-ups, we should do the same to other people. If we hold something against someone, that is something our old nature wants us to do — the same nature Paul just finished telling us to put off.

Other aspects of our old nature which Paul says to put off are wrath, blasphemy (ungodly speech, which includes profanity), and filthy language. Filthy language includes not only swearing, but, more importantly, murmuring, griping and complaining.

Murmuring, griping and complaining does not change a situation for the better. All it usually does is give Satan an opportunity to cause confusion in the Body of Christ. God was ready on several occasions to wipe the children of Israel out of existence because of their constant murmuring and complaining, and it was only through the intercession of Moses that they were spared. We should learn a valuable lesson from that.

Instead of murmuring, griping, and complaining about a situation, we should pray and get in agreement about it. That is what will change the situation for the better. When you gripe, murmur or complain, it means you are not trusting God, and that you are doubting and questioning God's leadership. It is as much as saying to God, "You do not know what you are doing."

Lie Not

Paul adds this in Colossians 3:9:

Do not lie to one another....

Jesus said, **"I am the way, the truth, and the life,"** not the lie. If you are a Christian, you are as much Jesus Christ as Jesus Christ is Jesus Christ, because you are a member of the Church, otherwise known as the Body of Christ.

If people kept that concept in mind, they would not treat other people the way they do sometimes, because they know Jesus would not treat them that way. That includes lying. You may not be perfect, but you can be truthful.

Colossians 3:9-10:

Do not lie to one another, since you have put off the old man with his deeds, and have put on the new man who is renewed in knowledge according to the image of Him who created him.

In order to renew, you need the knowledge — knowledge of the Word of God. Without that knowledge, you will gravitate to doing things which are God-dishonoring and faith-destroying — things which actually give comfort to the enemy. That is what makes the knowledge of the Word so important. Once you get that knowledge, you can act on it.

James 1:21:

Therefore lay aside all filthiness and overflow of wickedness, and receive with meekness the implanted word, which is able to save your souls.

James says it a little differently than Paul does, but the message itself is the same — take off the old man, and all the attitudes and actions associated with him that are not consistent with the Word of God, and put on the new man. The responsibility for doing that is yours, whether or not your body feels like doing it. God is not going to do it for you, because He has given you everything you need to get it done, through the Word and the victory you have in Christ Jesus. In fact, God expects you to do it, because He knows you are well able. All you have to do is want to do it, stand on God's Word, and go from there.

Lie 5
Homosexuality Is Normal

There is a considerable amount of discussion these days about homosexuality, especially in these days of increased media attention and public accommodation of the "gay" lifestyle. Various lobbyist groups promote legislation that places homosexuality in a legally more favorable light. Situations and conditions formerly frowned upon have now almost gained common acceptance.

Also, some doctors have conjectured that a person's homosexuality is determined by his or her genetic make-up. They have asserted there is no way a man can determine whether he will be sexually attracted to other men or to women, or a woman to other women or to men, though they have had no conclusive hard evidence on which to base their assertions, and the number of cases they have had in their studies have been at best extremely limited.

What does God have to say about the subject? I believe that in His care and concern for mankind, He has given us some guidelines for living, through His Word, that can be as helpful today as they have been throughout the ages. Most of our present conditions in society, when you look closely at them, are really fresh variations on old themes. This includes the subject of homosexuality. Let us see what the Bible says about this controversial topic, and determine from that how it measures up in terms of its being normal and acceptable in God's eyes.

Before I go any further, let me clarify why I am discussing this subject. Personally, I have no "axe to grind," and nothing to gain from taking on the issue of homosexuality. But Jesus Himself said that the truth will make us free, and that is all I want to do — set people free by teaching them the Word of God and letting them make informed decisions from there.

Also, John 3:16 says, **"For God so loved the world that He gave His only begotten Son, that whoever believes in Him should not perish but have everlasting life."** *Whoever* includes homosexuals and lesbians. God cares enough about homosexuals to make salvation through Jesus available to them, and He loves them enough to make them His children. However, love includes being totally honest, whether or not a person really wants to hear what you have to say.

Is Homosexuality Natural?

Paul writes in Romans 1:21-27:

> because, although they knew God, they did not glorify Him as God, nor were thankful, but became futile in their thoughts, and their foolish hearts were darkened.
> Professing to be wise, they became fools,

and changed the glory of the incorruptible God into an image made like corruptible man — and birds and four-footed animals and creeping things.

Therefore God also gave them up to uncleanness, in the lusts of their hearts, to dishonor their bodies among themselves,

who exchanged the truth of God for the lie, and worshiped and served the creature rather than the Creator, who is blessed forever. Amen.

For this reason God gave them up to vile passions. For even their women exchanged the natural use for what is against nature.

Likewise also the men, leaving the natural use of the woman, burned in their lust for one another, men with men committing what is shameful, and receiving in themselves the penalty of their error which was due.

Notice, in the last two verses, that Paul uses the word *natural*. That is a very interesting and provocative term. The direct opposite of natural is unnatural — in other words, what is not natural. This indicates that in the sight of God, some things are considered natural, and some are considered unnatural.

For instance, your ears were designed for hearing. They also house the balancing apparatus for the body, so that is a natural use of the ear. You can also use them to hang earrings on. But your ears were not designed for that purpose, so you could consider wearing earrings to be unnatural. Whether that makes it right or wrong depends on the effect earrings have on your ears.

To my knowledge, there is no case history of a person's hearing being adversely affected by the wearing of earrings. It does not usually cause a problem with the conscience of the wearer. That cannot necessarily be said for unnatural uses of other organs of the body. Some of these uses can cause damage to the body. Some of them can put a person in a state of depression or confusion, or engender a moral crisis that may cause that person to seek counseling to determine if what he or she is doing is permissible behavior. The unnatural uses which can engender all these things include homosexual intercourse.

Think about it. What is a penis for? What is a vagina for? What is the anus for? When it comes to sex — or anything else, for that matter — if there is any reservation, embarrassment, or guilt, or any feelings of unworthiness or of being dirty, chances are that something is out of order.

Every organ of the body has a purpose, and when you violate that purpose, the body cannot function in that area, or at least function as it should. If you damage your ears and can no longer hear through them, there is no other organ in your body you can hear with. Likewise, when you violate your body in other ways, there is a price to pay for it.

Here is something else to consider. If it were natural for men to be sexually attracted to other men, and women to be sexually attracted to other women, it would be possible for two men or two women to produce a baby. This is not the case. Women are the only human beings who can conceive children, and men are the only human beings who can fertilize the egg of the woman. Therefore, homosexuality cannot be natural. It has to be against nature.

Choices and Influences

Some homosexuals or lesbians may think I am being narrow-minded, that I am just another preacher who is "down" on homosexuality. They may share the opinion one young man had when he wrote a letter to me about being homosexual. In his letter, he said, "You do not have any real feeling for us. It is not fair. You should understand us and our lifestyle."

After reading that letter, I asked the Lord to help me understand. After all, I did not invent homosexuality. I did not put the terms *natural* and *against nature* into the Bible. Those expressions were there when I started studying the Word many years ago.

Let's read Romans 1:26-27 again, and I will show you what the Holy Spirit revealed to me to help me understand.

> For this reason God gave them up to vile passions. For even their women exchanged the natural use for what is against nature.
> Likewise also the men, leaving the natural use of the woman, burned in their lust for one another, men with men committing what is shameful, and receiving in themselves the penalty of their error which was due.

Paul says in verse 26, ... **For even their women exchanged the natural use....** He adds in verse 27, **Likewise** [or in the same manner] **also the men, leaving the natural use....** The fact that they changed shows that those men and women were **not** the same way at **birth**, and that they had a choice as to whether or not to change. Otherwise, they would never have left **the natural use** in the first place. The Bible clearly states it is people who change. No person can blame his homosexuality on the environment, on his parents, or even on the way he was born.

Now, I am the first to admit that we can be influenced by our surroundings and other people. We are all bombarded with influences, from the time we are children. But we do not have to yield to those influences. Our yielding to them is a matter of choice. A man who is a woman-chaser is that by choice. He was not born that way. He simply let his body govern and control him. There have been times, in counseling sessions, when I have been propositioned, and my body has been tempted to give in. I knew it would be wrong, and that getting away with it would not make it right, so I resisted that urge.

We all have the capacity to resist temptation. Even Jesus was tempted to sin, and He resisted. Paul writes in Hebrews 4:15, **For we do not have a High Priest who cannot sympathize with our weaknesses, but was in all points tempted as we are, yet without sin.** For Jesus to be tempted, He had to be able to succumb to that temptation. Otherwise, it is not a temptation. If someone offers me a million dollars to get pregnant and have a baby, I can easily say no, because there is no way I can become pregnant. I do not have the physical equipment with which to become pregnant, so it is not a temptation.

According to Paul, Jesus **was in all points tempted as we are.** For that to be true, He had to be tempted with lying, stealing, drugs, alcoholism, fornication, adultery and homosexuality, among other things. He had the ability to give in to all those things, and He did not do so. He was **tempted in all points as we are, yet without sin.** If Jesus was tempted to sin and did not do so, that means we do not have to yield when temptation comes, either.

The issue is really not whether or not you have a desire to do something, or that you are tempted to do it. The real issue is what you do with that desire. You can choose whether or not to yield to temptation, just as I had the opportunity to choose whether or not to break my marriage vows and offend God.

Consider the same principle on this situation. We just read in Romans 1:26 and 27 that the people chose to follow unnatural desires. That also means a person can choose to resist an unnatural desire, just as I can resist committing adultery. That person can control the urge. The urge should not control the person. A man's physical attraction to another man or a woman's attraction to another woman is not justification to act upon that urge.

When You Yield

In case a person still wants to yield to those urges, Paul tells us this in Romans 1:28:

> And even as they did not like to retain God in their knowledge, God gave them over to a debased mind, to do those things which are not fitting.

According to this verse, the person with a debased mind is hindered when it comes to making judgments. And you have to make judgments: I will do this, I will not do that. If you do not make some sound decisions, you stand a good chance of doing some or all of **those things which are not fitting** listed in Romans 1:29-31:

> being filled with all unrighteousness, sexual immorality, wickedness, covetousness, maliciousness; full of envy, murder, strife, deceit, evil-mindedness; they are whisperers,
> backbiters, haters of God, violent, proud, boasters, inventors of evil things, disobedient to parents,
> undiscerning, untrustworthy, unloving, unforgiving, unmerciful.

Paul adds in verse 32:

> who, knowing the righteous judgment of God, that those who practice such things are deserving of death, not only do the same but also approve of those who practice them.

When you do something that is blatantly wrong, you generally know it is wrong at the time you do it, and you have something nagging at you from the inside, bugging you about it. Many people call these promptings "unctions" or "conscience," but in reality, it is the voice of your spirit.

Even an unsaved man is still a spirit; he has a soul, and he lives inside a physical body. The only difference between him and a Christian is that the unsaved man has not made Jesus his personal Savior and Lord. However, your spirit has no more power to make you do right or do wrong than the traffic signal on the corner has the ability to make you stop. You can very easily drive through an intersection when the signal advises you to stop, and you may hit another car or a pedestrian when you do so, but that is not the signal's fault. The responsibility lies solely with you.

It is also possible to "sear" your conscience — to harden your spirit so that you do not hear what it is saying any more — just like you harden the outside of a steak by searing both sides to seal the meat's juices in. Your spirit is still inside you, giving its warning, but you may have trampled over it so much that you do not pay any more attention to it.

Here is something else in verse 32 to consider:

> **who knowing the righteous judgment of God, that those who practice such things are deserving of death....**

Paul does not say here that God will kill you for doing those things. God has nothing to do with murder, sickness, disease, or anything else that can wipe you out. He is not the author of AIDS, HIV, or any other sexually-transmitted disease. All God wants to do is forgive you and take care of you as His child. That is why He made salvation available to us through Jesus. However, our continuing to act on "those things which are not fitting" will open the door for negative things such as murder, sickness and disease to come into our lives. That is what God means when He says through Paul **that those who practice such things are deserving of death.**

God does not want you to die, but He will allow death to take you, just as He allows you to do the things which can eventually kill you. God gave you a free will, and He will not violate that will. However, He wants to let you know what can happen to you, so you will be informed. From that point, you are responsible for the decisions you make, and the consequences that arise from them. God will allow you to succumb to complications of AIDS, but it is not His choice. It is yours.

What Paul says in Romans 1:32 is not limited to sinners, either. Christians are just as subject to Paul's admonition as sinners are. Many Christians fornicate and commit adultery. Many act maliciously and enviously. Many gossip and do everything else listed in Romans 1:29-31. And it is making them sick and killing them.

Sure, Sin Can Be Fun, But ...

Some people enjoy homosexuality and lesbianism. But the fact those things give pleasure does not make them right or ordained by God. In fact, Proverbs 9:17-18 tells us, **"Stolen water is sweet, and bread eaten in secret is pleasant." But he does not know that the dead are there; that her guests are in the depths of hell.** That is extremely similar to what we read in Romans 1:32, about the people who act on these things being **deserving of death.**

You may engage in homosexuality because you feel it is part of your inborn nature. That is Satan feeding false thoughts into your mind. You are not born with those desires, but you can be that way if you choose. Perhaps, deep down inside, you know it is not right. But because you have gotten away with it, and because it seems more people are doing it now than 10 or 15 years ago, you figure it must be all right.

According to the Bible, something bad is going to happen to you sooner or later if you continue in sin. God is not the one who will do it to you, but He loves you and cares about you enough to tell you the truth. Homosexuality is a sin, just as much as murder, lying, or stealing. Sin is sin, hell is hell, and the lake of fire is the lake of fire. God says in Romans 6:23 that the wages of sin is death.

Personally, I do not think any worse of the homosexual than I do of the adulterer, and from what I have gathered from my study of the Bible, neither does God. He loves the sinner, and wants that person to turn his or her life over to Jesus. If there is something in your past or your personality you cannot deal with alone, you can come to the Lord Jesus Christ, and by the power of God through His Holy Spirit, He will help you. If you truly want to be free, Jesus is the answer. Whether or not you accept that as your answer is entirely up to you.

Lie 6
Thank God for Everything, No Matter What

The Apostle Paul tells us in Ephesians 5:20, **giving thanks always for all things to God the Father in the name of our Lord Jesus Christ.** On the surface, this verse would seem to say that we should thank God for everything that happens to us. But are we really supposed to always give thanks for all things to God, no matter how good or bad that thing may be?

That is what some people would tell you. For many years, the idea of thanking God for everything, no matter what, was a very popular teaching in the Christian community.

What stymied me when I first heard this teaching promulgated was that I would have to thank God for every good thing *and every bad thing* that happened to me. It would mean that if I had a relative who was an alcoholic, unsaved, and was hit by a car and went to hell, I would have to thank God for that. It would mean that if some Christian who served God and for all intents and purposes lived a godly life was stricken with cancer at an early age and died from it, I would have to thank God for it. That person was too young to die! Nevertheless, I would have to say, "Praise the Lord! Thank you, Lord, that this person died of cancer."

I certainly am in agreement with the fact that if a person takes a positive attitude and thanks God for everything that happens to him, he will be the better for it mentally. However, it does not do credit to the Heavenly Father, and it does not do credit to the Word of God to take that attitude, even though you may be the better for it in terms of being able to handle the situation. In short, it is not what the Word of God tells us to do.

Rendering What Is Due

Read Ephesians 5:20 one more time, and allow me to point out something the Spirit of God revealed to me.

> **giving thanks always for all things to God the Father in the name of our Lord Jesus Christ.**

Notice the words *to God*. It would be simple to give thanks for all things to the Heavenly Father in Jesus' name, so why emphasize *to God*? Those two words are the key here.

In Matthew 22:15-21, we have an incident recorded that clarifies why *to God* is so important.

> **Then the Pharisees went and plotted how they might entangle Him [that is, Jesus] in His talk.**

88

> And they sent to Him their disciples with the Herodians, saying, "Teacher, we know that You are true, and teach the way of God in truth; nor do You care about anyone, for You do not regard the person of men.
>
> Tell us, therefore, what do you think? Is it lawful to pay taxes to Caesar, or not?"
>
> But Jesus perceived their wickedness, and said, "Why do you test Me, you hypocrites?
>
> "Show me the tax money." So they brought Him a denarius.
>
> And He said to them, "Whose image and inscription is this?"
>
> They said to Him, "Caesar's." And He said to them, "Render therefore to Caesar the things that are Caesar's, and to God the things that are God's."

Verse 21 alerts us to the fact that not everything is Caesar's, and not everything is God's. It tells us that we should not give Caesar credit for what God has done. A second verse that directly connects with this idea is Romans 13:7:

> Render therefore to all their due: taxes to whom taxes are due, customs to whom customs, fear to whom fear, honor to whom honor.

What we are told to do in Matthew 22:21 and Romans 13:7 is to make a value judgment of all the things that happen to us. We are to evaluate those things, and determine whether or not those things are Caesar's, and whether or not they are God's. If they are Caesar's, we should give Caesar credit for them. If they are God's, we should give God credit for them.

Caesar, Who Is Really ...

I am sure you realize that actually, there are only two personages or two forces we really have to contend with in our Christian walk — the forces of God, and the forces of Satan. We really do not have to deal with Caesar as such, yet I believe that in this story, Caesar really represents the powers of Satan, and we can read Matthew 22:21 this way:

> "... Render therefore to Satan the things that are Satan's, and to God the things that are God's."

In 1 John 3:8, this is further elucidated:

> He who sins is of the devil, for the devil has sinned from the beginning. For this purpose the Son of God was manifested, that He might destroy the works of the devil.

That means there must be such a thing as a devil, even though certain religious groups say he does not exist. Not only that, but if Jesus was manifested to destroy the works of the devil, then the devil must have some works, as well. Otherwise, there would have been no works for Jesus to destroy, and He would have wasted His time by coming into the earth realm.

The word *destroy* here does not mean to obliterate or wipe out something. If it did, there would not be any more works of the devil. All you have to do is look around at all the mess in the world today to know that is not true.

In the original Greek, *destroy* is the word *luo*, and it means "to loose or set free from." What that implies in the context of this verse is, because of sin, mankind was bound by satanic influence and was limited in its ability to move and act freely. Jesus came into the world to set men free. Once a person accepts Jesus as his personal Lord and Savior, the sin and the power of Satan that restricted his life is broken, and he is set free from it.

The Devil's Works

Now that we know the devil has works, what kind of things would be classified as works of the devil? Since the Bible tells us there are works of the devil, we can expect it will categorically list for us what those things are. That way, we will be able to tell whether something is a work of God or a work of the devil, and not blame God for something the devil did, or vice versa.

In John 10:1-10, Jesus gives us the M.O. (modus operandi) of both God and the devil:

> "Most assuredly, I say to you, he who does not enter the sheepfold by the door, but climbs up some other way, the same is a thief and a robber.
> "But he who enters by the door is the shepherd of the sheep.
> "To him the doorkeeper opens, and the sheep hear his voice; and he calls his own sheep by name and leads them out.
> "And when he brings out his own sheep, he goes before them; and the sheep follow him, for they know his voice.

"Yet they will by no means follow a stranger, but will flee from him, for they do not know the voice of strangers."

Jesus used this illustration, but they did not understand the things which He spoke to them.

Then Jesus said to them again, "Most assuredly, I say to you, I am the door of the sheep.

"All who ever came before Me are thieves and robbers, but the sheep did not hear them.

"I am the door. If anyone enters by Me, he will be saved, and will go in and out and find pasture.

"The thief does not come except to steal, and to kill, and to destroy. I have come that they may have life, and that they may have it more abundantly.

"I am the good shepherd. The good shepherd gives his life for the sheep."

Jesus says, **"I am the good shepherd."** We can therefore consider ourselves to be the sheep. The thief, who comes to steal the sheep, is the devil, because the devil is the only person interested in stealing the sheep. He is the avowed foe and antagonist of God.

In verse 10, Jesus says He came so we might have life, and have it more abundantly. Abundant life does not include things being stolen from you. It does not include having things destroyed, or having you killed. Jesus says the thief is the one who comes for those purposes. Therefore, anything that steals, kills, or destroys is of the devil, and God does not have anything to do with it!

Jesus uses a very loaded term when He says, **"The thief does not come except to steal, and to kill, and destroy."** A thief does not come to your front door, ring the doorbell, and say, "Good morning! I'm here to rob your house." He tries to be as unobtrusive as possible, in a place where he is not exposed, because if he is exposed, he is taking a chance of being caught.

Jesus says in Luke 12:39, **"But know this, that if the master of the house had known what hour the thief would come, he would have watched and not allowed his house to be broken into."** The thief comes when you least expect him, when you are not looking for him. That means it is possible for the thief to steal, kill and destroy if you are not constantly on your guard. In the case of the Christian, "on your guard" means keeping watch with the Word of God and weighing everything accordingly.

Thank God ... for Everything?

Keep in mind what we have read about the works of God, the works of the devil, and rendering honor or blame to whom honor or blame is due, and read Ephesians 5:20 once more.

> **giving thanks always for all things to God the Father in the name of our Lord Jesus Christ.**

As I said at the beginning of this chapter, the key words here are *to God*. As I said before, if you are going to thank God for every blessing and every calamity that befalls you, the words *to God* are unnecessary here.

However, thanking God for every blessing and every calamity is NOT what this verse is telling us to do.

Rather, it is telling us to give thanks to God for the things God does for us — **for all things to God,** or, in other words, for all things that are God's. That also means that if we are going to give God thanks for everything He does for us, we should not give Him thanks for what the devil has done! We should not thank God that someone is sick, poor, dying, or dead.

First Thessalonians 5:18 is another scripture like Ephesians 5:20, and on the surface, it would seem to contradict what I have just said. Remember, though, that the Bible instructs us to be diligent to show ourselves approved unto God, rightly dividing the Word of truth. God is not the author of confusion, and many times what may at first seem confusing or contradictory is not really that way once we look at it in detail, especially concerning the things of God.

First Thessalonians 5:18 says this:

> in everything give thanks; for this is the will of God in Christ Jesus for you.

When they read this verse, many people think, "You see! It *does* say to thank God for everything!" You may have thought the same thing yourself. However, that is not what this verse is saying at all.

If you read this verse very carefully, you will notice that it does not say, "*For* everything give thanks" — or, if you turn it around, "Give thanks *for* everything." It does not say, "*For.*" It says, **In everything give thanks.** In other words, "Give thanks *in* everything." We are supposed to give thanks in sickness, in poverty, in adversity. We are not supposed to give thanks *for* those things, but while those things are happening to us, we are to give thanks.

If that is the case, what are we supposed to give thanks *for* while these things are happening to us?

If we are sick, for example, we are supposed to give thanks that, according to 1 Peter 2:24, with Christ's stripes we were healed, and we do not have to accept sickness! We are supposed to give thanks that ... **He Himself took our infirmities and bore our sicknesses** (Matt. 8:17). We are supposed to give thanks that the Lord Himself said, **"... I am the Lord who heals you"** (Exod. 15:26).

Instead of thanking God for whatever calamity Satan throws against us, we should stand on the Word and thank God for the solution He promises us in His Word for that challenge! In the face of situations which seem to tax us beyond human abilities, we can rely on God as our source, because His Word says in Philippians 4:13, **I can do all things through Christ who strengthens me.** That means we can rise in the middle of that situation, flex our spiritual muscles, snatch Satan and demons by the neck, and cast them out of our circumstances!

When a negative situation arises, I can say, "Praise God," and thank God right in the middle of it. I do not have to rely on myself, because the Bible says I have the Greater One living in me, and that Jesus has been made unto me wisdom, knowledge, and sanctification through the Holy Spirit. I can do anything through Christ, so I can give thanks in any situation. I do not have to say, "Oh, I hope this doesn't happen." I have the Greater One inside of me, and He has all the answers.

When the economic wolf is at the door, and the prices at the supermarket are going up faster than my paycheck, I can give thanks, because Philippians 4:19 says, **And my God shall supply all your need according to His riches in glory by Christ Jesus.** I do not praise God that the prices are going up. I say, "Praise God that I can still go into the store and buy anything I need, because my Father is my source, not my pocketbook!"

What about temptations, trials, and tests? There is no way you can get around them, and no place where you will not be tempted, tried, or tested in this earth realm. You do not give thanks for the temptation, trial, or test. It is never nice when it happens, it does not feel good, and there is nothing in the temptation, trial, or test in itself to be thankful for.

However, you can give thanks that 1 Corinthians 10:13 says, **No temptation** [trial or test] **has overtaken you except such as is common to man; but God is faithful, who will not allow you to be tempted** [tried or tested] **beyond what you are able, but with the temptation will also make the way of escape, that you may be able to bear it.** We can say, "Praise the Lord that I don't have to stay in this thing," push the eject button, and, in the name of Jesus, bail out of the trial.

The latter part of this scripture should also prove without a shadow of a doubt that God is not the one who tests, tries, or tempts you. God knows human nature, and He knows we will always take the path of least resistance, so if He gives us an escape route, it defeats any purpose He may have in trying us.

Therefore, it must be the thief, the murderer, and the robber — Satan — who brings the temptation, trial, or test. All God gives us is the way out.

Do we thank God for everything? NO! We thank God for what God has done. We will have to have accurate knowledge of the Word, so we can know the M.O. of the devil and the M.O. of the Father. That way, we can give the devil his due, give God credit for what He has done, and walk from there to victory after victory in Christ Jesus.

Lie 7
God Is Glorified
Through Sickness

If you have been a Christian for any length of time, chances are that you may have heard one of these statements: "I'm sick for the glory of God"; "God is teaching me something through this sickness"; "God's trying to get my attention, so He put this sickness on me"; or, "Well, it's true that when Jesus and the apostles walked the earth, they did perform miracles and heal people. However, those things are not for us today."

Many leading ministers have made a big to-do about the idea that God makes people sick for His glory, that the way He gets glory from His children is by having them afflicted with some disease or other malady. It sounds reasonable when you examine Church history or denominational history, because there have been so many Christians who have been sick.

However, that idea, and all the statements I have quoted, come as a result of ignorance of what the Bible says about sickness, diseases, and healing. God says in Hosea 4:6, **"My people are destroyed for lack of knowledge."** We can paraphrase that and say, "My people are destroyed because they are ignorant of My Word." And guess who wants you ignorant so he can destroy you? I guarantee you that the answer is not God.

To answer the question, "Is God glorified through sickness," we must first establish from the Bible what the origin of sickness is. We must always recognize that the Word of God must be the final line of defense — not my opinion, your opinion, or whatever you heard, but what the Word says. If God created the universe and keeps it running flawlessly, then He certainly knows what He means in His Word.

In the thirteenth chapter of the gospel of Luke, we have a situation outlined which clearly presents the origin of sickness and disease.

Luke 13:10-12:

> Now He [Jesus] was teaching in one of the synagogues on the Sabbath.
>
> And behold, there was a woman who had a spirit of infirmity eighteen years, and was bent over and could in no way raise herself up.
>
> But when Jesus saw her, He called her to Him and said to her, "Woman, you are loosed from your infirmity."

Jesus does not say, "You are loosed from your blessing." He does not say, "You are loosed from the glory of God." He says, **"You are loosed from your infirmity."** An infirmed person, in common language, is

100

someone who is not functioning up to par physically or mentally. That person is impaired in his or her ability to function as a physical organism.

Now notice something very important in the next verse.

Luke 13:13:

> **And He laid His hands on her, and immediately she was made straight, and glorified God.**

Right there, if we did not go any further, that punches a sizable hole in the balloon of those people who have been saying, "I'm sick for the glory of God." This lady had been bound for 18 years, and the first thing that pops out of her mouth when she is healed is, "Praise the Lord! Glory to God!" Verse 13 says she glorified God.

If we are to believe God gets the glory out of people being sick, this is a strange turnabout. Apparently, during those 18 years she was bound, this lady was not saying, "Glory to God." If she had already been saying, "Glory to God," there would be no need to say anything now.

Luke 13:14:

> **But the ruler of the synagogue answered with indignation, because Jesus had healed on the Sabbath; and he said to the crowd, "There are six days on which men ought to work; therefore come and be healed on them, and not on the Sabbath day."**

Beware! The Lies of Satan

Wasn't this ruler a loving, kind, compassionate individual? Here was a woman who for 18 years could not lift herself up and is finally set free from her infirmity, and all this man can say is, "Well, you did it on the Sabbath day" — much like some preachers today who never read the Bible and get indignant because you do not do things their way.

Notice very carefully how Jesus answered the ruler in the next two verses. The point He makes is extremely important to what we are discussing here.

Luke 13:15-16:

The Lord then answered him and said, "Hypocrite! Does not each one of you on the Sabbath loose his ox or donkey from the stall, and lead it away to water it?

"So ought not this woman, being a daughter of Abraham, whom Satan has bound — think of it — for eighteen years, be loosed from this bond on the Sabbath?"

Jesus wanted it clearly understood that God did not get in on any of the binding of this woman. Jesus said the woman was bound by the devil those 18 years. For the entire time she was bowed together and could not lift herself up, it was the work of Satan, not the work of God. This directly ties in to what the Apostle Peter says in Acts 10:38, which effectively sums up Jesus' three-and-a-half-year ministry in the earth realm.

> "how God anointed Jesus of Nazareth with the
> Holy Spirit and with power, who went about doing
> good and healing all who were oppressed by the
> devil, for God was with Him."

"And healing all that were oppressed by the devil...." This statement must refer to everyone Jesus healed. Otherwise, it does not tell us about the entire healing ministry of Jesus. Therefore, we can conclude that sickness and disease is satanic oppression.

If anyone ought to know Jesus' attitude about sickness and disease, it should be Peter. Peter was one of "the big three" — Peter, James and John. These three disciples were Jesus' high command, so to speak. Any time a major decision had to be made or a new direction had to be taken, Jesus would call aside Peter, James and John. For the three and a half years they traveled with Him, they were His right-hand men.

> "how God anointed Jesus of Nazareth with the
> Holy Spirit and with power, who went about doing
> good and healing...."

Healing must be good, since Peter says, **Who went about doing good and healing....** If healing is good, sickness must be bad; and if sickness is bad, it cannot come from God, because God is not bad! The Bible says that God is love, and there cannot be anything bad in love. In fact, on one occasion when someone ran up to Jesus, kneeled before Him and called Him "Good Teacher," Jesus said, "Why do you call Me good? No one is good but One, that is, God."

How God Is Glorified

We now have two witnesses, Jesus and Peter, who say sickness and disease does not come from God, but from Satan. That fulfills the scriptural prerequisite for proof, since the Bible says in 2 Corinthians 13:1, "By the mouth of two or three witnesses every word shall be established." Since sickness and disease is from Satan, we do not have to accept it.

Now the question becomes, "Is God glorified through sickness, or is He glorified through healing?" To answer that, we will examine some scriptures, and see if any of them actually make reference to the idea that God is glorified through sickness. The first verses of scripture we will read are found in the ninth chapter of John, in the celebrated case of the man who was born blind.

John 9:1-2:

Now as Jesus passed by, He saw a man who was blind from birth.

And His disciples asked Him, saying, "Rabbi, who sinned, this man or his parents, that he was born blind?"

It is interesting that the disciples did not ask, "Did God make this man blind?" They were spiritually astute enough to recognize that blindness, maladies and crippling diseases do not come as a result of doing good, but of doing evil. Now notice how Jesus answers their question.

John 9:3:

> Jesus answered, "Neither this man nor his parents sinned, but that the works of God should be revealed in him."

"See, Brother Price! The man was born blind for the work of God." That is what this verse can appear to say if you read it like that, and that is the way it appears to be written in the New King James Bible. But is that what it really *says*?

I submit to you that it is not what this verse says at all. You must realize that in the original Greek manuscripts from which our English Bibles were translated, the text was written in all capital letters, with no small case designations, punctuation marks or verse designations. The small case, verse designations and punctuation marks were not ordained by God as such, or inspired by the Holy Spirit, but were added by the translators to render reference points and bring clarity to the writings.

Sometimes a punctuation mark can change the whole meaning of a word and the context of the verse where the word is located. John 9:3 is a case in point. I would like to suggest, for your consideration, a changing of some punctuation marks. I will not change the words which were ordained by God, but only the punctuation marks which were added by man.

John 9:1-2:

> Now as Jesus passed by, [comma] He saw a man who was blind from birth. [period]

**And His disciples asked Him, [comma] saying,
[comma] "Rabbi, [comma] who sinned, [comma] this
man or his parents, [comma] that he was born blind?
[question mark]"**

The disciples asked Jesus a two-fold question. They
were saying, in essence, "The man is blind — we can see
that. What we want to know is what caused it. Did this
man sin [because the Jews believed a baby could sin
inside its mother's womb], or his parents, that he was
born blind?" Jesus had to give them one of three specific
answers — "The man," "His parents," or "Neither
one" — because they asked Him a specific question.

John 9:3:

> **Jesus answered, "Neither this man nor his par-
> ents sinned, but that...."**

I believe there should be a period here following
the word *sinned* instead of a comma. A period would
indicate that the disciples' question had been
answered. End of discussion, right?

Then Jesus went one step further. However, in
order to understand the step, we have to capitalize one
word, and change a period to a comma.

Let's read this verse again:

John 9:3-4:

> **Jesus answered, "Neither this man nor his par-
> ents sinned, but that the works of God should be
> revealed in him.**

"I must work the works of Him who sent Me while it is day...."

Now, by changing the comma after *sinned* to a period, and capitalizing the word *but*, we have an entirely different story. It would read like this:

Jesus answered, "Neither this man nor his parents sinned. [period]"

As I said earlier, that answered their question, didn't it? Capitalize the word *but*, and we have,

"But that the works of God should be revealed in him, [change the period to a comma] I must work the works of Him who sent Me...."

Can you see what a difference a punctuation mark makes? Jesus says, "But that the works of God should be manifest in him, I must work the works of Him who sent me." He then set about doing the work. What was the work of God? To make the man see!

If it were the will of God that the man be blind, then Jesus interrupted the will of God by healing the man. Not only that, but it would have contradicted the Word of God, because in John 14:10, Jesus says He is not the one doing the works, but the Father who is in Him. How could God, who was in Jesus, first make the man blind, then heal the man from his blindness? God would be working against Himself.

It was God's will for that blind man to be healed, just as it is His will for every blind person to be healed today!

At the Tomb of Lazarus

Another scripture which can appear to say that God is glorified through sickness, and which has also been misinterpreted, is in the story of the raising of Lazarus in John 11.

John 11:1-4:

> Now a certain man was sick, Lazarus of Bethany, the town of Mary and her sister Martha.
> It was that Mary who anointed the Lord with fragrant oil and wiped His feet with her hair, whose brother Lazarus was sick.
> Therefore the sisters sent to Him, saying, "Lord, behold, he whom You love is sick."
> When Jesus heard that, He said, "This sickness is not unto death, but for the glory of God, that the Son of God may be glorified through it."

Someone may read that and say at this point, "You see, Brother Price! Jesus very plainly says it. This man was sick for the glory of God."

That is not what Jesus is saying at all.

The beginning of verse four says, **When Jesus heard that, He said, "This sickness is not unto death...."** In essence, what Jesus was saying is, this sickness will not terminate in death, but it will terminate in the glory of God. In other words, the end result of this sickness would not be death. The end result would be the glorifying of God.

Later in this chapter, Jesus came to the town where Mary and Martha were. Lazarus had been dead four days from the sickness, and Jesus went out to the tomb where he was buried. Remember that Jesus had said the end of the sickness would not be death, but the glorifying of God.

John 11:39-40:

Jesus said, "Take away the stone." Martha, the sister of him who was dead, said to Him, "Lord, by this time there is a stench, for he has been dead four days."
Jesus said to her, "Did I not say to you that if you would believe you would see the glory of God?"

If the sickness that apparently terminated in death was for the glory of God He had talked about four days before, Jesus would have to leave Lazarus in the grave, because God was getting glory out of this man being dead. If He brought him out of the grave, God would not get any more glory out of it, because that man would not be dead any more.

John 11:41-42:

Then they took away the stone from the place where the dead man was lying. And Jesus lifted up His eyes and said, "Father, I thank You that You have heard Me.
"And I know that You always hear Me, but because of the people who are standing by I said this, that they may believe that You sent Me."

Jesus does not say, "I thank you that you are about to hear me," or "I thank you that you are hearing me now." He says, **"I thank You that You have heard Me."** That is past tense. When did God hear

Him? Four days before, praise God, when He said, **"This sickness is not unto death, but for the glory of God."**

One of the key references here, and one of the key principles in the operation of faith in the kingdom of God, are the words Jesus Himself says in Mark 11:23: **"For assuredly, I say to you, whosoever says to this mountain, 'Be removed and be cast into the sea,' and does not doubt in his heart, but believes that those things he says will be done, he will have whatever he says."**

Jesus desired that what would bring God glory would come to pass. For that reason, He stood at that grave and said, **"Father, I thank You that You have heard Me. And I know that You always hear Me, but because of the people who are standing by I said this, that they may believe that You sent Me."**

John 11:43-44:

Now when He had said these things, He cried with a loud voice, **"Lazarus, come forth!"**
And he who had died came out bound hand and foot with graveclothes, and his face was wrapped with a cloth. Jesus said to them, **"Loose him, and let him go."**

"The glory of God" Jesus mentioned was for Lazarus to be well, not to die. Again, if the glory of God were for Lazarus to be sick and die, Jesus should have left him in the tomb. But Jesus did not do that.

A Minimum of 70 Years

Another scripture we will look at is in Luke 7, namely the story of the widow of Nain's son.

Luke 7:11-14:

> Now it happened, the day after, that He went into a city called Nain; and many of His disciples went with Him, and a large crowd.
> And when He came near the gate of the city, behold, a dead man was being carried out, the only son of his mother; and she was a widow. And a large crowd from the city was with her.
> When the Lord saw her, He had compassion on her and said to her, "Do not weep" [in other words, do not cry].
> Then He came and touched the open coffin, and those who carried him stood still. And He said, "Young man...."

Notice, Jesus did not say, "Old man." He said, **"Young man."** The fact He says, **"Young man"** means this man had not lived out his full life. Under the Old Covenant, the children of Israel were promised a minimum of 70 years. If a person died before he turned 70, he was actually cheated out of years he should have had on the earth.

Luke 7:14-16:

> Then He came and touched the open coffin, and those who carried him stood still. And he said, "Young man, I say to you, arise."

> So he who was dead sat up and began to speak. And He presented him to his mother.
>
> Then fear came upon all, and they glorified God....

They glorified God. Why do you think they did that? Because the young man was raised.

Luke 7:16:

> Then fear came upon all, and they glorified God saying, "A great prophet has risen up among us"; and, "God has visited His people."

Isn't that something? When life came, the people said, **"God has visited His people."** That must mean when death comes, it must not be God — especially if a person's life is terminated before he reaches the minimum number of years.

Let me clarify something. I realize physical death is here, and that everyone will physically die if Jesus does not come back before that time. The Bible very plainly states in Hebrews 9:27, ... **it is appointed for men to die once, but after this the judgment.**

However, the wise man who is instructed in the Word and knows how to walk by faith recognizes that, though it is appointed for men to die once, he is the one who should be making the appointment, after he has lived at least 70 years and is fully satisfied with his life, not before.

Your Body, the Temple of God

In each of the cases we have read, God received the glory when someone was healed, not when that person was afflicted. You will not find a scripture that contradicts this, because if you do, that will mean God is the author of confusion — and the Bible emphatically states that God is not the author of confusion. In fact, if you read through the four Gospels and the book of Acts, you will find many more instances which confirm what I have just said.

If you are still not convinced that God is not glorified through sickness, notice what Paul says in 1 Corinthians 6:19-20:

> **Or do you not know that your body is the temple of the Holy Spirit who is in you, whom you have from God, and you are not your own?**
> **For you were bought at a price; therefore glorify God in your body and in your spirit, which are God's.**

How can you glorify God in your body when it does not function right? The Bible says your body is the temple of the Holy Spirit. What makes you think God wants to live in a body where He cannot see through the eyes or hear through the ears, or where the limbs, organs and cells do not function correctly? You would not want to live in a house with a leaky roof, the toilet running over and the electricity not working. Why treat God differently? If He lives in a body that does not function properly, He will be limited, not helped.

The Blessing of Abraham

We looked at this before, but I want us to reread Luke 13:10-16, because there is something extremely important in these passages of scripture which we did not point out before.

> Now He was teaching in one of the synagogues on the Sabbath.
> And behold, there was a woman who had a spirit of infirmity eighteen years, and was bent over and could in no way raise herself up.
> But when Jesus saw her, He called her to Him and said to her, "Woman, you are loosed from your infirmity."
> And He laid His hands on her, and immediately she was made straight, and glorified God.
> But the ruler of the synagogue answered with indignation, because Jesus had healed on the Sabbath; and he said to the crowd, "There are six days on which men ought to work; therefore come and be healed on them, and not on the Sabbath day."
> The Lord then answered him and said, "Hypocrite! Does not each one of you on the Sabbath loose his ox or donkey from the stall, and lead it away to water it?
> "So ought not this woman, being a daughter of Abraham, whom Satan has bound — think of it — for eighteen years, be loosed from this bond on the Sabbath?"

Jesus said the devil had the woman bound, and that, because she was a daughter of Abraham, she ought to be loosed.

It is interesting to note why Jesus said the woman was a daughter of Abraham. God had established a covenant with Abraham, and there is what is called the blessing of Abraham. That blessing, which is outlined in the 28th chapter of Deuteronomy, includes the fact that the people who operate under the blessing would have divine health, and sickness could not raise its ugly head under their roofs. It said if they followed the Word of God and lived under His commandments, God would take sickness out of the midst of them.

The Bible says we are the seed, the spiritual children, of Abraham. Because of that, we are entitled to the blessing of Abraham. The Apostle Paul tells us in Galatians 3:13-14:

> Christ has redeemed us from the curse of the law, having become a curse for us (for it is written, "Cursed is everyone who hangs on a tree"),
> that the blessing of Abraham might come upon the Gentiles in Christ Jesus, that we might receive the promise of the Spirit through faith.

He also says this in verses 28 and 29 of the same chapter:

> There is neither Jew nor Greek, there is neither slave nor free, there is neither male nor female; for you are all one in Christ Jesus.
> And if you are Christ's, then you are Abraham's seed, and heirs according to the promise.

Jesus said this woman was a daughter of Abraham. But she perhaps did not know her covenant rights — just like people today do not know their rights in Christ Jesus. Satan took advantage of her ignorance

115

and put an affliction on her for 18 years. If Jesus had not come along, she probably would have died from that sickness, but thank God that Jesus came.

Paul mentions another important point in Galatians 3:7:

Therefore know that only those who are of faith are sons of Abraham.

Are you of faith? If you are not of faith, that means you are not saved. Every Christian has to be of faith, because, as Ephesians 2:8 points out, **For by grace you have been saved through faith....** If you are of faith, you are a child of Abraham, spiritually speaking, and you are an heir of everything Abraham was an heir to.

Whatever the promise to Abraham was, we should have it, too! In fact, the Bible says we have a better covenant than the one the woman operated under, established upon better promises. For our covenant to be better, it has to have everything the old one had, and more. If that woman could be healed under the Old Covenant, then we should be healed under the New Covenant.

Is God glorified through sickness? Not according to the Bible. God is glorified through healing and divine health, because then He can function through us without any hindrance to His glory. Yes, we will still be attacked with sickness, because we are always in a state of spiritual warfare with the devil and his forces. But we do not have to accept sickness when it comes. We can stand against it on God's Word, and keep on going without so much as breaking stride.

Lie 8
Being Poor Is Being
Humble for the Lord

There are many forms of prosperity. For instance, I occasionally get letters from husbands and wives about how their lives have changed as a result of coming into contact with the Word. The things said in those letters are indicative of prosperous marriages. Other forms of prosperity can include social prosperity, mental prosperity, physical prosperity in terms of your health, educational prosperity and professional (job-related) prosperity.

The peculiar thing is, no Christians, ministers, theologians, or denominations have any problem with those aspects of prosperity. The only aspects of prosperity they criticize and attack are financial and material prosperity. When you start talking about them, all the worms come out of the woodwork.

It is obvious why this happens. Because Satan dominates the Church in terms of the world economic system, the Church in general does not have the resources it needs to fully proclaim the Gospel around the world. It costs money to build church buildings, to equip them, to provide pastors, send out missionaries, and do everything else we must do to get the Word out into the world.

Who else is going to pay for all this, besides the children of God? No one. Satan knows that, and if he keeps us poor, we will have limited resources to give into the Church. You can support something only to the degree that you give into it, and Satan definitely does not want the Church to prosper.

Satan also knows that by keeping us poor, he keeps us defeated. There is certainly more to the Christian life than material things. But let's face it — we have to live a spiritual life in the context of a physical environment, and it costs a considerable amount of money to do so. Just to keep food on the table, clothes on your back and a roof over your head can be horrendous on your pocketbook, especially if you are supporting a family. If you are constantly wondering where the money to pay the month's rent or the grocery bill will come from, you will not be able to give to the kingdom like you should or to even concentrate on the things of God so you can grow spiritually.

This is why Satan has so cleverly infiltrated theology and passed off the following idea: If you are a Christian, you are supposed to be spiritual. However, if you are spiritual, you are not supposed to have any financial or material wealth. If you are doing more than "just scraping by" financially or materially, you are not being spiritual, and you are missing God.

This is not what the Bible says at all!

Many people, Christians and non-Christians alike, often get on the preacher's case when he starts talking about money. It is true that we have had some crooked ministers, but you have crooks everywhere. There are crooked politicians in government, crooked doctors practicing medicine, crooked lawyers arguing court cases. There are crooked wives, crooked husbands, crooked boyfriends, girlfriends, children and parents.

Are you going to shut down government, or all the doctors' offices and hospitals, or all the courts, because some of the people who work there are dishonest? Of course not. It is conceivable that you have some preachers who are not right, but it is not fair to cast all ministers in the role of being dishonest.

Christians need to learn about material and financial prosperity for two reasons. First, they need to learn about it so they can take care of their own needs. Second, they need to learn about it so they can help finance the spreading of the Gospel.

Chicken dinners, barbecues, bake sales, and bingo games will not bring in enough money to finance what the Church has to do, and all those things are not God's way of financing the kingdom. God's way is by prospering the people to the extent that they can be channels of blessing, and that through them, He can get the Church the resources it needs. As Deuteronomy 8:18 puts it:

> **"And you shall remember the Lord your God, for it is He who gives you power to get wealth, that He may establish His covenant which He swore to your fathers, as it is this day."**

Salvation is only the beginning of that covenant. I believe the totality of it is exactly what Jesus said when He told the disciples, **" I have come that they may have life, and that they may have it more abundantly"** (John 10:10). God's covenant with man is abundant life.

However, you cannot have that abundance or function in God's financial plan until you know and believe God wants you to prosper. Do not go through the syndrome of thinking, "The Lord did not want me to have this, and God may get me if I get too much of that." That is a trap of the devil. God wants you to succeed in every area of living, and that includes materially and financially.

How You Become Prosperous

In Joshua 1:8, read the following:

> "This Book of the Law shall not depart from your mouth, but you shall meditate in it day and night, that you may observe to do according to all that is written in it. For then you will make your way prosperous, and then you will have good success."

"This Book of the Law shall not depart from your mouth" simply means you should never stop speaking God's Word. **"But you shall meditate in it day and night"** means that God's Word ought to be a part of your everyday life.

The reason you should meditate on God's Word day and night is **"... that you may observe to do according to all that is written in it."** It is not enough to just observe, but you have to do it — act on it — as well. When you do that, **"... then you will make your way prosperous, and then you will have good success."**

Notice that it does not say, "... for then God will make your way prosperous." It says you will make your way prosperous. You are responsible for your prosperity, because God has already done all He is going to do about it. No gold will fall out of the sky tomorrow. Oil will not rain down from the heavens. All the wealth is in the earth-realm, so you have to do something about it.

"For then you will make your way prosperous, and then you will have good success." The reason God says to have good success is that it is possible to have bad success, as well. If you are making $10,000,000 a year and your child is on drugs, you are not having good success. Having your family torn asunder is not good success. Having those things that make you miserable is certainly not good success. Your net worth may tell people you are successful, but if you have no peace of mind, forget it. That is the type of success God is telling you to avoid.

That does not mean God is telling us not to be successful. On the contrary. God wants us to prosper and to have good success. In fact, whether you know it or not, God actually rejoices in our prospering! Psalm 35:27 tells us this:

> Let them shout for joy and be glad,
> Who favor my righteous cause;
> And let them say continually,
> "Let the Lord be magnified,
> Who has pleasure in the prosperity of His servant."

The opposite of pleasure is displeasure, and the opposite of prosperity is poverty. Therefore, if God has pleasure in the prosperity of His servant, He must have displeasure in the poverty of His servant.

Blessed Is the Man ...

Another passage of scripture that tells us about prosperity is the First Psalm. What makes it important is not only that it tells us we should be blessed, and in which ways we should prosper, but it also gives us a checklist of things to make sure about ourselves before God's financial plan can work for us. The first three verses tell us the following:

> **Blessed is the man**
> **Who walks not in the counsel of the ungodly,**
> **Nor stands in the path of sinners,**
> **Nor sits in the seat of the scornful;**
> **But his delight is in the law of the Lord,**
> **And in His law he meditates day and night.**
> **He shall be like a tree**
> **Planted by the rivers of water,**
> **That brings forth its fruit in its season,**
> **Whose leaf also shall not wither;**
> **And whatever he does shall prosper.**

Whatever he does includes raising your kids. It includes your marriage, your sex life with your spouse, your business, your ministry. Whatever you are involved in is supposed to prosper. This is exactly what the Apostle John tells us when he says, **Beloved, I pray that you may prosper in all things and be in health, just as your soul prospers** (3 John 2).

For **whatever he does** to prosper, however, you have to meet all the conditions set forth in verses one and two.

> **Blessed is the man**
> **Who walks not in the counsel of the ungodly....**

You have to be walking right.

> **Nor stands in the path of sinners....**

You cannot be fellowshipping with sinners — living with them, shacking up with them, going into business with them — and expect this to work.

> **Nor sits in the seat of the scornful....**

You cannot be scornful or act or talk scornfully and have this verse work for you.

> **But his delight is in the law of the Lord....**

"The law of the Lord" here means the Word of the Lord. That is what you should delight in. You may delight in comic books, in a slam-dunk, in a soap opera, but your delight should be in knowing and acting upon God's Word.

And in His law he meditates day and night.

When we hear or read the word *meditate*, we usually picture sitting down and quietly thinking. This word in the Hebrew really means "to mutter, mumble" — to speak, in other words. You should be speaking the Word day and night, as well as thinking about it, if you are doing what this verse says. The bottom line is, God wants you to prosper, and He is trying to tell you here how to do it.

A Tree Planted

When you are meditating in the Word day and night, verse three says you **shall be like a tree planted....** This verse could have said, **He shall be like a tree,** and that would have been good enough. But it says, **... a tree planted.**

One day, I was driving along the freeway to officiate at a wedding, and next to me was a diesel big-rig truck pulling a huge tree on a flatbed trailer. The box that contained the root system and the dirt was sitting next to the cab of the truck, and the rest of the tree went all the way to the back of the trailer. That tree was not planted. It was not drawing any nutrients from the ground, and it was not producing any fruit.

What is so important about being **like a tree planted by the rivers of water** is that it can draw water from under the ground and be sustained. The person who is like this tree **brings forth its fruit in its season, whose leaf also shall not wither.**

You will not do those things if you are not "planted" in God's Word, but once you are planted, ... **whatsoever he does shall prosper.** This ties in with Joshua 1:8, when God says we will prosper when we meditate on His Word continually, and observe to do what the Word says. *Prosperity is the natural outcome of meditating in and doing what the Word says.* The prosperity will take care of itself, but you cannot be prosperous God's way without meditating in and doing the Word. If you put a pan of water on the stove and turn the burner on, the water's boiling is automatic, but if you never put the pan of water on the burner, you will never have boiling water. Prospering God's way follows the same logic.

Abraham — Our Role Model

We will read from the third chapter of Galatians next to look at a role model God gives us for our prosperity. Why do we look for role models? Because they inspire us. We see someone who is successful, and it encourages us to think that perhaps we can be successful also. We do that many times with people in the world, but God has given us role models in His Word. All we need is the wisdom to ferret them out and learn from them.

Galatians 3:13-14:

Christ has redeemed us from the curse of the law, having become a curse for us (for it is written, "Cursed is everyone who hangs on a tree"),

that the blessing of Abraham might come upon the Gentiles in Jesus Christ, that we might receive the promise of the Spirit through faith.

Abraham is used in the Bible as an example and symbol of a man of faith. He is, in fact, called the Father of the Faithful. We who have been made children of God through Christ Jesus have received our salvation and our sonship with God through faith. We are faith people.

Galatians 3:7:

> **Therefore know that only those who are of faith are sons of Abraham.**

You would think this verse would say we are children of God, since God became our spiritual Father once we were saved. It says we are children of Abraham because God is using Abraham as a role model of a man of faith. God came to Abraham and said such-and-so and so-and-so, and Abraham believed Him. Abraham did not have any evidence to back up what God said. In fact, all of Abraham's evidence was to the contrary — but he believed God in spite of that. God gave him credit for being a righteous man, and called him a man of faith.

Now notice what verse nine says:

> **So then those who are of faith are blessed with believing Abraham.**

That should settle the argument once and for all. We are of faith, because the Bible says, **By grace you have been saved through faith.** Therefore, according to

Galatians 3:9, we are blessed along with Abraham. All we have to do is find out how Abraham was blessed, and we will know how we are supposed to be blessed.

How Abraham Was Blessed

We could speculate on how Abraham was blessed, but that would not make any difference when the enemy comes in like a flood. Many times, the devil talks people out of things because they do not have a good foundation in the Word of God. You can believe what I or any other minister says about a subject, but when it is time to do battle with demon forces, you cannot say, "Thus saith Pastor So-and-so ..." and expect to win. If you use anything but what the Lord says about a subject, you will promptly get your backside kicked.

What is much better, and what we will do now, is to read what the Word of God has to say about how Abraham was blessed, and go from there. That way, we will know that we know what to expect from God.

Genesis 12:1:

> **Now the Lord had said to Abram:**
> **"Get out of your country,**
> **From your family**
> **And from your father's house,**
> **To a land that I will show you."**

Let me make a point here. God is a God of the family. To the children of God, He is not called God, but Father. The Father God is in the business of creating and unifying the family.

However, notice the very strange situation outlined in Genesis 12:1. God told Abraham to get out of his father's house, get away from his familiar surroundings, leave his city and country, and go to a place He would show him. That is a tall order.

If God is a God of the family, why would He tell Abraham to do this? It would seem to contradict what God normally stands for, but the reason He told Abraham to leave is actually simple.

Sometimes, if you are going to walk in the ways of the Lord, you will have to leave at least some of your family. They will not understand what you are doing, and if you stay with them, they will drag you down to their level. It can be heart-rending. It can be traumatic. But you now have a choice — please the family or please the Heavenly Father.

However, "If you are willing and obedient," as the Bible says in Isaiah 1:19, "you shall eat the good of the land." Not only will you eat the good of the land, but God will give you a bigger family than the one you may have to leave. He will give you so many family members that you will not be able to count them — people who will protect you, stand up for you, fight for you, love you and take care of you. Sometimes the people in your new family will be better than the people in your blood family, because they will love you with the love of God, not just with a selfish blood-love relationship.

Now remember that we read in Deuteronomy 8:18 — "And you shall remember the Lord your God, for it is He who gives you power to get wealth, that He may establish His covenant" — and notice what God says to Abraham in Genesis 12:2:

> "I will make you a great nation;
> I will bless you
> And make your name great;
> And you shall be a blessing."

If God had said, "I will make you a great nation; I will bless you," and stopped there, that would have been great. But God does not stop there. He also says, "And you shall be a blessing." God blesses people through people. However, you cannot give what you do not have. That was why He told Abraham, "I will bless you and make your name great; and you shall be a blessing."

Genesis 12:3:

> "I will bless those who bless you,
> And I will curse him who curses you;
> And in you all the families of the earth shall be blessed."

God never said that to anyone else. Abraham is the man God used to get back into the earth realm. God had given Adam dominion over all the resources He had created, but Adam gave that dominion over to the devil. Therefore, God had to have another man by which he could get back into this world, and get that blessing back to the people of God. So He did it through Abraham. Through Abraham's descendants, Jesus eventually came on the scene, and through Jesus, we are blessed with salvation and all other things pertaining to life and godliness. But it started with Abraham.

How did God bless Abraham? According to Genesis 13:1-2:

> **Then Abram went up from Egypt, he and his wife and all that he had, and Lot with him, to the South.**
> **Abram was very rich in livestock, in silver, and in gold.**

Abraham was not just rich. He was *very* rich. How was he very rich? **"In livestock, in silver, and in gold."** Thank God that God Himself tells us how Abraham was blessed, so that no person can mess it up. Nobody can say, "That's just spiritual, Brother Price," because that is *not* what this verse says. It says he was very rich in livestock, silver and gold. Those are material things!

Still, Genesis 13:1-2 does not say this was the blessing that God gave Abraham, per se. Just to make sure God was the one who was blessing Abraham, let us look at another passage of scripture.

In the 24th chapter of Genesis, there is a story about Abraham sending his servant out to find a wife for his son Isaac. His servant went out and really did not know where to go. He prayed for God to direct him to the right place, and God led him to the part of the country where Abraham's relatives were located.

The servant then asked God to send the right person to come offer him and his camels water, and it happened exactly as the man had prayed.

Genesis 24:29-35:

> Now Rebekah had a brother whose name was Laban, and Laban ran out to the man by the well.
> So it came to pass, when he saw the nose ring, and the bracelets on his sister's wrists, and when he heard the words of his sister Rebekah, saying "Thus the man spoke to me," that he went to the man. And there he stood by the camels at the well.
> And he said, "Come in, O blessed of the Lord! Why do you stand outside? For I have prepared the house, and a place for the camels."
> · Then the man came to the house. And he unloaded the camels, and provided straw and feed for the camels, and water to wash his feet and the feet of the men who were with him.
> Food was set before him to eat, but he said, "I will not eat until I have told about my errand." And he said, "Speak on."
> So he said, "I am Abraham's servant.
> "The Lord has blessed my master greatly, and he has become great; and He has given him flocks and herds, silver and gold, male and female servants, and camels and donkeys."

The servant said, **"The Lord has blessed my master greatly"** — not just blessed him, but blessed him greatly. He then enumerated exactly how God had blessed Abraham. All the things he listed were not spiritual things. They were material things.

How the Servant Knew

Let me ask you a simple question, and share with you a revelation the Lord gave me. The servant said it was God who blessed his master Abraham, but who told the servant that it was the Lord who had given it to him? We have no indication that the servant was a worshiper of Jehovah, so how did he know?

The servant more than likely knew because Abraham told him. That means Abraham probably testified about where and how he got his wealth.

This may seem simple, but to me, it was a great revelation, and it gave me more proof for the way God has led me to minister, in terms of sharing what He has done in my life. When I started walking in faith, God began to call my wife and me to go to various places. When we returned home, I would show my children the honorariums I received for ministering and tell them, "This is what the Lord did."

Because I did this, my children grew up knowing that everything their parents had came from the Lord, and they learned by example the biblical precept that you can serve God and prosper. They saw you can serve God and do everything legitimately, honestly, aboveboard, and still achieve in this society, but that you have to do it God's way.

The reason I shared what the Lord did for me with my kids was that I wanted them to prosper and be successful in everything they do in life. It is the same reason I tell my congregation, when I teach, how God has blessed me and my family. It opens me up to criticism, but that does not bother me. All that matters is that people find out they do not have to "pull strings" or do things "under the table" to get ahead, and that they can use what the Bible says about prosperity to get where God wants them to be.

One thing people forget is, when God prospers you, it gives you a powerful witnessing tool. When other people see you in a beat-up car, or no car, wearing raggedy clothes, chances are they do not want to hear you talk about Jesus. They will take one look at you and figure, "If I have to go through what he's going through with all this Jesus stuff, forget it."

On the other hand, when you pull up to the curb in a Rolls-Royce and get out wearing a custom-tailored business suit, people want to know quickly how you got it. When a financially successful person like that starts sharing how the Lord blessed him, even heads of state and presidents of major corporations will become interested — and those are the people who should be included when we witness. We have traditionally ignored them, and have concentrated on the man on the street, but Jesus died for the corporate head and the man on the street, for the rich, the poor, and everyone in between.

Do not let anyone tell you material wealth is of the devil. It is not. It is used by the devil, but it does not come from him. It comes from God, and the people who should have it are the people of God. God made the herds, the flocks, the silver and the gold. Satan did not create them — God did. He created them for Adam

133

and Adam's seed, which includes Abraham, and we are Abraham's seed by the same faith that made us children of God. That means He created them for *us*.

Seeking First, Then Having Added

Someone may say at this point, "I don't know, Brother Price. If I get ahold of all the things I need, I don't know if I will stay committed to the Lord. After all, those things can really mess you up."

That is really a confession of ignorance. First of all, the Bible says to **"... seek first the kingdom of God and His righteousness, and all these things shall be added to you."** As we have pointed out in several other scriptures, you have to be seeking the kingdom before the things are added to you.

Second, the things themselves are not necessarily bad. We are told in James 1:17 that **Every good gift and every perfect gift is from above, and comes down from the Father of lights, with whom there is no variation or shadow of turning.** God does not give you anything intrinsically bad. It is what you do with them that makes them bad.

Notice what Jesus says about this situation in Matthew 6:19-23:

> **"Do not lay up for yourselves treasures on earth, where moth and rust destroy and where thieves break in and steal;**
> **"but lay up for yourselves treasures in heaven, where neither moth nor rust destroys, and where thieves do not break in and steal.**

"For where your treasure is, there your heart will be also.

"The lamp of the body is the eye. If therefore your eye is good, your whole body will be full of light.

"But if your eye is bad, your whole body will be full of darkness. If therefore the light that is in you is darkness, how great is that darkness!"

Verse 21 is the key to this whole section. If you do not understand what you are reading, you can very easily think what Jesus is saying is for you not to have a bank account, and that you should not save money. That is NOT what God is saying here. Besides, if these verses were talking about earthly wealth, how could you lay up earthly wealth in heaven? You cannot, even though verse 20 tells us we should **"lay up ... treasures in heaven."**

Notice: **"For where your treasure is, there your heart will be also."**

The issue here is not treasure. The issue here is heart.

The word *treasure* is used in reference to earth and in reference to heaven. However, it is not referring to treasure as we think of treasure, but to the thing our hearts long after. Treasure to some people is sports. To other people, treasure is artwork, or music, or movies. Treasure is whatever you give your time to.

God wants us to put spiritual things first, because that is where He wants our treasure to be. Your heart will be wherever your treasure is, whether it is a heavenly treasure or an earthly treasure, and God wants us to get our hearts established in the right place!

Once your heart is established, everything else will follow suit. You cannot have a right heart and a wrong lifestyle, because Jesus says, "... a tree is known by its fruit." Whatever is inside your heart will come out in your behavior. If your treasure is in earthly things, your conduct will not be commensurate with the things of God, and the sole pursuit of your life will be the acquisition of material things.

This does not mean we cannot have wealth or material things. After all, God has them. Among other things, the Bible says He has a golden city. He simply wants us not to allow those things to have control over us.

If we continue to seek first the kingdom of God and His righteousness, we will not allow material things to control us. We will know that God's purpose for blessing us is not for us to hang onto what we receive, but to use those things as a tool to do the will of God. In other words, the more you follow God's plan, the more God will bless you.

Our Heavenly Father is not opposed to prosperity. Abraham was blessed because he was obedient to God. That was what put him in a position to prosper. God later told the children of Israel if they would be willing and obedient, they would eat the good of the land. They were not the born-again children of God, but the servants of Jehovah.

How much more is He saying to us as His children? If we are obedient, we will eat the good of the land. We will be in a position to help finance the proclaiming of the Gospel, and we will help establish the covenant God has sworn to give us. That is the plan and purpose of God where financial and material prosperity is concerned. To what extent you succeed depends on you and how closely you follow the plan He has given us in His Word on how the children of God are to prosper.

Lie 9
Tithing Is Not for the Church Today

In our last chapter, we established the fact that God wants us to be prosperous in every area of our lives — spiritually, soulishly, and physically — and that it includes financial and material prosperity. We found out that God has two purposes for prospering us financially and materially: first, to meet our own needs; second (and more importantly), to finance the proclamation of the Gospel. God wants us to prosper as individuals. And in our prospering, the family of God will prosper.

We also discussed the fact that the traditional idea of Christians "suffering" in poverty until either they physically die or Jesus returns is a deception the devil has spread to keep born-again Believers from wanting to prosper. A similar lie, which we will expound on in this chapter, concerns how God's financial plan is activated in a person's life. The lie is, that the concept of tithing is not for the church today, that it was something only the children of Israel were told by God to do. This is definitely not the case, as we will prove from the Word. Giving tithes and offerings is actually what gets God involved in our finances.

Tithing Before the Law of Moses

As I just said, tithing did not originate with the Law of Moses. We can see this fact revealed in Genesis 14:13-20:

> Then one who had escaped came and told Abram the Hebrew [that is, Abraham], for he dwelt by the terebinth trees of Mamre the Amorite, brother of Eshcol and brother of Aner; and they were allies with Abram.
> Now when Abram heard that his brother was taken captive, he armed his three hundred and eighteen trained servants who were born in his own house, and went in pursuit as far as Dan.
> He divided his forces against them by night, and he and his servants attacked them and pursued them as far as Hobah, which is north of Damascus.
> So he brought back all the goods, and also brought back his brother Lot and his goods, as well as the women and the people.
> And the king of Sodom went out to meet him at the Valley of Shaveh (that is, the King's Valley), after his return from the defeat of Chedorlaomer and the kings who were with him.
> Then Melchizedek king of Salem brought out bread and wine; he was the priest of God Most High.
> And he blessed him and said:
>
> "Blessed be Abram of God Most High,
> Possessor of heaven and earth;
> And blessed be God Most High,
> Who has delivered your enemies into your hand."
>
> And he [Abram] gave him a tithe of all.

This incident took place approximately 430 years before the Law was given to Moses at Mount Sinai. It shows people were aware of tithing before the Law came into existence. Tithing was incorporated into the Law because, as we said earlier, tithes and offerings are God's methods through which He can bless His people financially and materially, and He wanted Israel to be blessed.

In the 28th chapter of Genesis, we have a follow-up to what we just read in the 14th chapter regarding tithing.

Genesis 28:10-14:

> Now Jacob went out from Beersheba and went toward Haran.
>
> So he came to a certain place and stayed there all night, because the sun had set. And he took one of the stones of that place and put it at his head, and he lay down in that place to sleep.
>
> Then he dreamed, and behold, a ladder was set up on the earth, and its top reached to heaven; and there the angels of God were ascending and descending on it.
>
> And behold, the Lord stood above it and said: "I am the Lord God of Abraham your father and the God of Isaac; the land on which you lie I will give to you and your descendants.
>
> "Also your descendants shall be as the dust of the earth; you shall spread abroad to the west and the east, to the north and the south; and in you and in your seed all the families of the earth shall be blessed."

This is exactly the same promise God gave to Abraham. Isaac and Jacob were the first and second

141

generations of the seed of Abraham, and what God had said to Abraham would come to pass through Isaac and Jacob.

Now notice what happens in the next several verses.

Genesis 28:15-22:

> "Behold, I [that is, God] am with you and will keep you wherever you go, and will bring you back to this land; for I will not leave you until I have done what I have spoken to you."
>
> Then Jacob awoke from his sleep and said, "Surely the Lord is in this place, and I did not know it."
>
> And he was afraid and said, "How awesome is this place! This is none other than the house of God, and this is the gate of heaven!"
>
> Then Jacob rose early in the morning, and took the stone that he had put at his head, set it up as a pillar, and poured oil on top of it.
>
> And he called the name of that place Bethel; but the name of that city had been Luz previously.
>
> Then Jacob made a vow, saying, "If God will be with me, and keep me in this way that I am going, and give me bread to eat and clothing to put on,
>
> "so that I come back to my father's house in peace, then the Lord shall be my God.
>
> "And this stone which I have set as a pillar shall be God's house, and of all that you give me I will surely give a tenth to You."

A tithe is a tenth. The word *tithe* means one tenth, or 10 percent. If it is not a tenth, it is not a tithe.

This incident also took place before the Law was given. The Bible says in Matthew 18:16, "... **by the mouth of two or three witnesses every word may be established,**" and here we have two instances which show that tithing was a known and practiced way of life before the Law of Moses was given.

Our High Priest, Jesus, Receiving the Tithe Today

At this point someone may think, "Well, what you are saying is right so far, Brother Price, but the Bible does not say anything about tithing today. After all, it says we are not under the Law, but under grace. That would include the law of tithing, would it not?"

That is not necessarily true. Tithing is mentioned in the New Testament. In the sixth and seventh chapters of the Book of Hebrews, the Apostle Paul emphasizes the fact that Jesus is the great high priest for the Body of Christ, and writes the following:

Hebrews 6:17-7:8:

> **Thus God, determining to show more abundantly to the heirs of promise [us] the immutability [or unchanging nature] of His counsel, confirmed it by an oath,**
>
> **that by two immutable things, in which it is impossible for God to lie, we might have strong consolation, who have fled for refuge to lay hold of the hope set before us.**
>
> **This hope we have as an anchor of the soul, both sure and steadfast, and which enters the Presence behind the veil,**

where the forerunner has been entered for us, even Jesus, having become High Priest forever according to the order of Melchizedek.

For this Melchizedek, king of Salem, priest of the Most High God, who met Abraham returning from the slaughter of the kings and blessed him,

to whom also Abraham gave a tenth part [in other words, a tithe] of all, first being translated "king of righteousness," and then also king of Salem, meaning "king of peace,"

without father, without mother, without genealogy, having neither beginning of days nor end of life, but made like the Son of God, remains a priest continually.

Now consider how great this man was, to whom even the patriarch Abraham gave a tenth [or a tithe] of the spoils.

And indeed those who are of the sons of Levi, who receive the priesthood, have a commandment to receive tithes from the people according to the law, that is, from their brethren, though they have come from the loins of Abraham;

but he whose genealogy is not derived from them received tithes from Abraham and blessed him who had the promises.

Now beyond all contradiction the lesser is blessed by the better.

Here mortal men receive tithes, but there he receives them, of whom it is witnessed that he lives.

Here mortal men receive tithes ... refers to the ministers of God here on earth, such as pastors. **There he receives them ...** is talking about Jesus. In Revelation 1:18, Jesus told the Apostle John, **"I am He who lives, and was dead, and behold, I am alive forevermore."** That ties in directly to what we just read in Hebrews.

Since He went back to heaven some 2,000 years ago, Jesus has acted as our high priest there. He has interceded for us and ministered in the heavenly sanctuary on our behalf. This includes offering up our tithes to the Heavenly Father.

The point is, if Jesus is supposed to be receiving tithes in heaven today, and the ministers in the earth realm are supposed to be receiving them also, it implies that we should be paying tithes. The verse does not say that Jesus and the ministers received tithes. It says they receive them, and *receive* is present tense.

The Storehouse

Malachi 3:10 says:

> "Bring all the tithes into the storehouse,
> That there may be food in My house,
> And try Me now in this,"
> Says the Lord of hosts,
> "If I will not open for you the windows of heaven
> And pour out for you such blessing
> That there will not be room enough to receive it."

The storehouse is God's house, the place set aside for the worship and praise of God and the study of His Word. In short, the storehouse is the local church. It takes money to maintain the storehouse, so if you are being spiritually fed at your local church, you should give that church your tithes.

Not every local church is going to be a storehouse, however. In Deuteronomy 26:14, there is a statement which is absolutely astounding in its import concerning what is and what is not a storehouse. The verse says this:

> "I have not eaten any of it [from the tithe] when in mourning, nor have I removed any of it for an unclean use, nor given any of it for the dead. I have obeyed the voice of the Lord my God, and have done according to all that You have commanded me."

In The Amplified Bible, the meaning of this verse is given even greater clarity.

> I have not eaten of the tithe in my mourning [making the tithe unclean], nor have I handled any of it when I was unclean, nor given any of it to the dead....

Unfortunately, there are many churches that are D-E-A-D! There is no life and no anointing in them.

If a church is not proclaiming the Word of God and meeting the spiritual needs of the people, it is dead. You have no business putting God's money in there, and if you put it there, you will be out of the will of God.

It is easy to determine if a place is really a store-house, and it does not take long. Just listen for a few minutes to what is being said. Listen to the songs being sung. Listen to the preacher. Listen to the announcements.

You can soon tell whether or not the Holy Spirit has first place there. If you cannot tell, you are in serious trouble, and need to check yourself out.

All, Not Part

Now let us go back to Malachi. The first part of Malachi 3:10 says, **"Bring all the tithes into the store-house"** — not part of it, but all of it. Christians sometimes have a tendency to split up their tithes, and send some of it to this ministry, some of it to that outreach, and some to their local church. If you did not have a church or local congregation to go to, and a television ministry or outreach program was meeting your spiritual needs, then it would be all right to send all your tithes to that ministry.

If you are being spiritually fed through a local church or congregation, however, it is an entirely different matter. In this case, your primary obligation is to that local church, and your tithes should go there. You can go ahead and send an offering to any other ministry that benefits you spiritually. That would be all right. But according to this verse, your tithes should not go there if you get the primary amount of your spiritual feeding somewhere else.

Another interesting point about the storehouse can be found in Malachi 3:8-9:

> **"Will a man rob God?**
> **Yet you have robbed Me!**
> **But you say,**

147

'In what way have we robbed You?'
[God tells us,] In tithes and offerings.
You are cursed with a curse,
For you have robbed Me,
Even this whole nation."

Notice that, in verse eight, tithes come first. It says, "... tithes and offerings," not "... offerings and tithes." Verse 10 then instructs, "Bring all the tithes into the storehouse." It says nothing about bringing all the offerings, so we do not have to put all our offerings there if we want to bless other ministries. However, all the tithe is to go into the storehouse.

The tithe, really, is God's money. Offerings are what we desire to give from our money above and beyond the 10 percent God gets. Our responsibility as children of God is to be good stewards of God's money, to make sure we invest it well. It is more than an obligation. It is an honor, stated very succinctly in God's Word when it says, "Honor the Lord with your possessions, and with the firstfruits of all your increase" (Prov. 3:9). That alone should make you proud to tithe.

The Curse of the Law

There is an awesome statement contained in Malachi 3:9 which in itself would be enough to prompt discussion about the question of "robbing God." It is a statement of almost terrifying import, one that has been ignored by the Church at large, much to the Church's detriment, and is the true reason for asking,

"Will a man rob God?" That statement is, **"You are cursed with a curse, for** [or because] **you have robbed Me...."**

I want to let that sink in a minute. It is where I missed it for many years and did not know it, and it is where many other sincere, God-loving, honest Christians are missing it today. You may be born-again, filled with the Spirit, and go to church regularly. You may read your Bible, attend Bible class, and witness to others about Jesus. You may do good things. Your motive may be right, yet you have financial problems. You and your spouse may be working, and you may have an extra job, but you are still barely making it.

Maybe it is because you are robbing God by not tithing, and because of that, you are cursed with a curse.

Before we go any further, let me make something extremely clear. God is not putting the curse on you. No way, no how. The curse entered the human race in the Garden of Eden when Adam sinned. It is all around you, operating all the time, but it does not have to get on you if you are operating under God's Word. Remember, God gave us His Word as an umbrella to protect us from the curse. The umbrella of God's Word does not stop the curse any more than an umbrella stops the rain from falling. What it does is stop you from getting wet — and that is what is important. The Covenant of God keeps you from being under that curse.

God wants you to be free, and the way He has made available for you to become free financially is through tithes and offerings. For this reason, it is worth whatever it costs you to get into God's financial plan.

Once you are in that plan, you cannot lose. Therefore, it would be a good idea to examine yourself and find out if you are robbing God.

Proverbs 3:9 states something else about tithing which cannot be stressed enough:

**Honor the Lord with your possessions,
And with the firstfruits of all your increase.**

This is not talking about spiritual things. It is talking about substance. You honor the Lord with your firstfruits. That is the tithe. Your tithe should come off the top. Some Christians make the mistake of figuring their tithes after they have paid everyone else. If you do that, I guarantee there will not be much left to pay the tithe. You have to remember that the tithe is first.

What You Should Not Do to Tithe

Now I realize that, because you perhaps did not know how to operate this way in the past, you may be in bad financial straits. You may be like I was, unable to tithe without cutting somebody out of the budget or not paying your bills altogether.

Do not make that mistake. When you skip paying a bill to give to God, you lose your witness. You tell the man you are a Christian, make an agreement with him to pay him for services rendered, then do not keep your word when the money is due. If you do not have enough money to pay God and the light bill, you are already overextended. Remember, tithing is for your benefit, not God's.

If you have not been tithing before now, you are already a God robber. So do not start tithing until you can afford to do it. If you do not pay a bill, you are robbing the people you were supposed to be paying. That is even worse than robbing God. God will forgive you, but many times, people will not.

The same holds true if you write a check in the morning, then go to the bank in the afternoon and deposit the money to cover the check. Suppose there is a traffic accident on the way to the bank, or something urgent comes up to keep you from getting there? You may not get to the bank in time to beat the check. In other words, you would be caught lying. That can also be detrimental to your witness, and it, too, can cut off your blessings.

Another "little fox that spoils the vines" is when you postdate a check and do not tell the person about it. If you tell the person that you would like to postdate the check, and that person agrees to it, then it is fine. You have made that person aware of the situation, and as long as he agrees to it, it is all right. Normally, you must have the money in the bank to cover the check at the time you write that check out. If you give someone a postdated check without telling him anything, you can cut your blessings off.

To me, the tithe is first, and everything else revolves around it. The only money I have to spend is the amount left over after I pay my tithes. Whenever I get some money, the first thing I think of is the tithe.

You have to get into that position, also, and you may have to do something to get to that place. You may have to do without some things so you can pay off some bills before being able to tithe, but once you escape the curse and start operating in God's blessings, it is well worth it.

Learn to cast your bread upon the waters, according to Ecclesiastes 11:1. Then, as it says, "... you will find it after many days." Start casting it out. At first, you may not see any results, but keep on casting with your heart right as you exercise your faith. After a while, you will look out and see that every wave coming in has a loaf of bread on it! Then you will rise above your financial circumstances. You will be a recipient, and then a repository for the blessings of God.

How to Bring the Tithe

In the 26th chapter of Deuteronomy, we have an illustration or outline of the procedures for tithing — in other words, how we are to bring and present our tithes. There is a procedure, a biblical admonition, as to how we are to bring our tithes to the Lord. The chapter begins with this statement:

> "And it shall be, when you come into the land which the Lord your God is giving you as an inheritance, and you possess it, and dwell in it."

We are told in the Bible that God has a land, an inheritance, a possession for His people. For the children of Israel, it was the Promised Land, a land that flowed with milk and honey, which would be their earthly dwelling place. Under the New Covenant, God also has a land. I do not mean when we die and go to heaven, but I mean in the here and now. Colossians 1:13 tells us this:

> **He has delivered us from the power** [authority and dominion] **of darkness, and conveyed us into the kingdom of the Son of His love.**

Every born-again Believer has been translated into the kingdom. If you are a Christian, you are in that kingdom now.

We need to make a qualification here. If you read through the Gospels, you will especially notice in the Gospel of Matthew the emphasis placed on the words *kingdom of heaven*. When you read the Gospel of John, instead of *kingdom of heaven*, you will see the phrase *kingdom of God*. Many Christians have the idea that the kingdom of heaven and the kingdom of God are synonymous, that they are two different terms for the same place. However, I submit to you that they are *not* the same.

The kingdom of heaven is future; it has not yet come. The kingdom of heaven will operate in this physical earth and will be a political system. It will be a theocracy (*theos* meaning God), a God-ruled government with a prime minister or king, Jesus Christ. He will be the agent of the kingdom in the earth realm. The system is called the kingdom of heaven because its place of origin will be heaven, but it will also operate in the earth realm.

The kingdom of God, on the other hand, is God's rule and reign in the entire universe — physically and spiritually. When we receive Christ as our personal Savior and Lord, we become citizens of that kingdom. In that kingdom, we have the dominion, authority and power of Almighty God to be victors over the circumstances of life. That kingdom flows with milk and honey.

We are in the kingdom of God right now, and we have the authority of the name of Jesus. We have the Word of God and a New Covenant that can provide us with everything we may need or want in line with that Word. That includes being blessed over and above what the Israelites had when they entered the Promised Land, since the Bible says we have a better covenant which was established upon better promises (Heb. 8:6).

Let us go through the next several verses of Deuteronomy 26, and see what else constitutes God's procedure for bringing the tithes.

Deuteronomy 26:2:

"that you shall take some of the first of all the produce of the ground, which you shall bring from your land that the Lord your God is giving you, and put it in a basket and go to the place where the Lord your God chooses to make His name abide."

Remember that Israel was primarily an agrarian society. The people were basically farmers and cattlemen.

They did not go to the factory or the office or punch a time clock. The things they had to offer were their crops and livestock — that was the sweat of their brow.

In a mechanized society such as ours, however, the sweat of our brow brings us the dollar — that is the fruit of our labor. You go to work and beat a computer keyboard or do some other job all day long, and at the end of the week you get a paycheck. Therefore, money is what we have to bring to the Lord as the fruit of our labor.

Deuteronomy 26:3:

"And you shall go to the one who is priest in those days...."

We read in the sixth and seventh chapters of the Book of Hebrews about Jesus being made a high priest for us after the order of Melchizedec. Paul also says in Hebrews 3:1, **Therefore, holy brethren, partakers of the heavenly calling, consider the Apostle and High Priest of our confession, Christ Jesus.**

Deuteronomy 26:3-4:

"And you shall go to the one who is priest in those days, and say to him, 'I declare today to the Lord your God that I have come to the country which the Lord swore to our fathers to give us.'

"Then the priest shall take the basket out of your hand and set it down before the altar of the Lord your God."

This is what Jesus does when you bring your tithes and offerings. He receives them. He takes them and sets them before the altar in the high sanctuary of heaven.

Deuteronomy 26:5-10:

"And you shall answer and say before the Lord your God: 'My father was a Syrian, about to perish, and he went down to Egypt and dwelt there, few in number; and there he became a nation, great, mighty, and populous.

'But the Egyptians mistreated us, afflicted us, and laid hard bondage on us.

'Then we cried out to the Lord God of our fathers, and the Lord heard our voice and looked on our affliction and our labor and our oppression.

'So the Lord brought us out of Egypt with a mighty hand and with an outstretched arm, with great terror and with signs and wonders.

'He has brought us to this place and has given us this land, "a land flowing with milk and honey";

'and now, behold, I have brought the firstfruits of the land which you, O Lord, have given me.' Then you shall set it before the Lord your God, and worship before the Lord your God."

In short, when they brought their tithes and offerings, the children of Israel looked back and made a confession. They looked back to Egyptian bondage, but then they traced their history from that bondage to their present place in the Promised Land, and they proclaimed the blessing and gave glory to God.

As I said, we have also entered into the land we were promised — the kingdom of God. Satan had us in bondage, our lives bound up in sin. Jesus came and set us free through what He did for us at Calvary, so we could enter into the kingdom of God.

We should make a similar profession to what the Israelites made, but in our case, we should go back and look at Calvary, because that was the place where our redemption began. We should also declare that we are in the land that flows with milk and honey, because that is where the Bible says we are right now. We ought to confess all this and praise the Lord for it.

Here is an illustration of the kind of confession you can make today as a child of God.

Heavenly Father, we profess this day to You that we have come into the inheritance which You swore to give us. We are in the land which You have provided for us in Jesus Christ, the Kingdom of Almighty God. We were sinners serving Satan; he was our God. But we called upon the name of Jesus, and You heard our cry and delivered us from the power of darkness, and translated us into the kingdom of Your dear Son.

Jesus, as our Lord and High Priest, we bring the firstfruits of our income to You, that You may worship the Lord our God with them. Father, we rejoice in all the good which You have given to us and our households. We have heard Your voice and have done according to all that You have commanded us. Now Father, as you look down from Your holy habitation from heaven, to bless us as You said in Your Word, we believe that we now receive those blessings according to Your Word. This is our confession of faith, in Jesus' name.

This is the kind of confession you can make to the Lord when you bring your tithes. How long should we make that kind of confession? Hebrews 10:23 tells us, **Let us hold fast the confession of our hope without wavering, for He who promised is faithful.** *Hold fast* means to hold tight and not let go. In other words, we should make this profession all the time.

Blessed Financially and ...

We read Malachi 3:10 earlier in this chapter, but I want us to reread it now and notice something else about it.

> **"Bring all the tithes into the storehouse,**
> **That there may be food in My house,**
> **And try Me now in this,"**
> **Says the Lord of hosts,**
> **"If I will not open for you the windows of heaven**
> **And pour out for you such blessing**
> **That there will not be room enough to receive it."**

Notice one very important point here. God actually challenges us to try or test Him. (The King James Bible uses the word *prove*.) God knew the great emphasis that would be placed on economics in this world, so He challenges us in the area closest to most people — their money. So the play is ours. We have the ball. How do we "make the touchdown"? By challenging God to bless us when we give tithes and offerings. In other words, with our money.

Notice also that God says He will open to us **"the windows of heaven."** *Windows* is plural. In the account in Genesis concerning the Flood, it says the fountains of the deep were broken up and the windows of heaven were opened, and it rained 40 days and 40 nights. That same kind of "flood" is referred to in Malachi. God will open the windows of heaven to bless you.

Being blessed financially is not the only thing God offers us through tithing. He adds this in Malachi 3:11:

> **"And I will rebuke the devourer for your sakes,**
> **So that he will not destroy the fruit of your**
> **ground,**
> **Nor shall the vine fail to bear fruit for you in the**
> **field,"**
> **Says the Lord of hosts.**

In every other area of the Christian life, God tells us to do something. James 4:7 instructs, **Therefore submit to God. Resist the devil, and he will flee from you.** Ephesians 4:27 says, **nor give place to the devil.** Mark 16:17 states, **In My name they will cast out demons.** Luke 10:19 challenges us to **trample on serpents and scorpions, and over all the power of the enemy.** But in Malachi 3:11, God says, **"I will rebuke the devourer for your sakes."**

Whether you know it or not, there is a devourer loose in the earth realm. In fact, 1 Peter 5:8 warns us, **Be sober, be vigilant; because your adversary the devil walks about like a roaring lion, seeking whom he may devour.** It does not matter to him whom he devours — he is after everyone, including you! It should be obvious from what is happening in the world around you.

However, God says He will rebuke this devourer for you, and keep him from messing you up. Remember, though, that this will happen only when you prove God by tithing. He says, in essence, "I will do it — I will get involved, if you will bring the tithes." That is the qualifier here. If you do not bring your tithes, you are not opening the door for God to become involved in your circumstances.

Once you allow God to operate, not only will He rebuke the devourer, but He will make sure the devil **"will not destroy the fruit of your ground."** God's involvement means you will be successful, that everything you set your hand to will prosper. It means your business does not have to fail. It means that if you plant crops, your crops will grow even if everyone else's dies.

In effect, God's being involved in your circumstances allows you to defeat the enemy on two sides. The Lord will blast him on one side, and you can walk on him, rebuking him and casting him out on the other side! How can you lose? There is nothing for you to do but to win!

While Making Sure the Thief
Does Not Steal Your Blessings

This does not mean you stop using your faith. God said He would rebuke the devourer for you, but even there, if you do not continue to keep your faith on the line, the enemy will take advantage of the situation and steal from you. A lack of faith on your part will tie God's hands, because God cannot act on your behalf if you are not operating in faith. While God is waiting on you to use your faith, and you are waiting on God to do something, the enemy will come in and steal the blessing that is rightfully yours.

Remember what Jesus said in John 10:10 about Satan. He said, **"The thief does not come except to steal, and to kill, and to destroy."** Satan is a robber, and he will take advantage of every chance you give him to take something from you, especially if you do not stand on your covenant rights. Remember also that all of your blessings start out in the spirit world. By an act of your faith, the blessing which starts out in the spirit world will manifest in the physical world as a material commodity.

Here is what Satan does. He and his henchmen — his angels and demons — are like the stagecoach robbers in the old cowboy movies who would cover their faces with bandannas and wait in the bushes until the stagecoach came, then stop the stage and take the strongbox with the money inside. The moment you put your tithes in, the return starts on its way from God. However, while it is coming down from the spirit world to the physical world — into the town where you live — Satan's henchmen are waiting at the end of town to waylay the stage and steal your blessing. Unless you have your faith escorting that blessing down, Satan's forces stop the stage, and you get nothing.

There are many Christians who have tithed on a regular basis but have had no change in their personal economic situation, and the scenario I have just described is exactly what has happened to them. They did not understand how to operate in faith, or understand that they had to believe God for the return even though they may have known what the Bible said about the windows of heaven blessing.

This is an extremely important point to comprehend. If you do not know how to operate in faith, you will not get the blessings. Even though God is pouring those blessings out, the devil will steal them, just like he will rob you of your health, your job, or anything else.

What you have to do is not give Satan a chance to steal from you. You must use your faith and stand against him. You must take the Word of God and claim your rights. Every time you give your tithe, you can say, "Father, in the name of Jesus, I believe that I receive the windows-of-heaven blessings. Satan, take your hands off my money and keep them off, in Jesus' name, for the Word says that you are rebuked from my finances for my sake." Then he cannot touch what is coming to you.

The devil stole from me until I realized what was happening. He has not stolen from me since, because I do not allow it to happen any longer. My blessings are coming in all the time. I have made it a point to invest much into the kingdom through tithes and offerings, and I know how to use my faith, so Satan cannot stop my blessings from coming.

20 Percent — the Penalty for Robbing God

There is one other way you can stop your blessing from coming. That is when you stop tithing once you have started. When you do that, you will fall back into the curse of the law. You will not be walking in God's Word, and as a consequence, you will have no immunity from the curse.

When I started tithing many years ago, it was before I learned about the mechanics of it. Like many people, I started tithing out of fear. The preacher said we ought to tithe, and he read the scripture, "Will a man rob God?" That shook me up because I had robbed other people of some things that belonged to them, and the police had put me in jail swiftly. I did not want to mess up with God and be put in His jail, wherever that was, so I started tithing, even though my finances were already in a mess. When I started giving 10 percent to the church, I barely had enough money left to pay the bills. I knew nothing about claiming the windows-of-heaven blessings. Finally, I stopped tithing.

I did not know that a curse would result if I did not follow the Word of God, so I could not figure out why nothing seemed to be working for me, financially. Every deal I made would seem to fall through.

Unfortunately, I did not realize that tithing and offerings are not for God's benefit, but for ours. All I had thought was, "There is no point in my giving God ten dollars if I make only a hundred! I will give him one dollar and use the other nine to pay some bills." Without knowing it, I was not only robbing God, but myself also, because it is through our giving that God has a channel through which to bless us in the area of material things.

God, in His infinite wisdom, knew we would be tempted not to pay our tithes, even after we knew that we should. For this reason, He has built a penalty clause into the contract. Not only was I robbing God, but I compounded the robbery by operating in the penalty for the robbery.

You may think, "You are trying to put me under conviction, put me under bondage and put me in a bag," because this is something many people do not know about, but that is not what I am attempting to do here. I am actually attempting to get you out of the bag, so you can get out of the financial quagmire you may be in, and get to the point of operating in the freedom God has provided for you. *That* is why I am sharing this with you.

The penalty I mentioned is found in Leviticus 27:30-31. For those of you who may say, "But that is under the Law of Moses, Brother Price," remember that tithing was in place well before the Law of Moses went into operation. Going by that frame of logic would mean that the penalty for taking the tithes for our own use was also in place before the Law went into effect.

Leviticus 27:30-31 says this:

> "And all the tithe of the land, whether of the seed of the land or of the fruit of the tree, is the Lord's. It is holy to the Lord.
> "If a man wants at all to redeem any of his tithes, he shall add one-fifth to it."

"One-fifth" is 20 percent. That means if you give back the tithes you have taken, you have to pay back the tithes plus 20 percent. It is much cheaper and easier to pay the tithe and not borrow from it in the first place. Again, I am not telling you this to put you in bondage, but to help you get out of whatever circumstances you may be in.

One point you may wonder about is, does this mean we should add one-fifth to the original amount of money the tithe was taken from, or the total tithe, or what?

It is talking about redeeming the tithe itself, not the money the tithe originally came from. For example, if I make $100 a week, my tithe would be $10. Let us say I decided to give $5 of the tithe and keep the other $5 to help pay a bill. If I took $5, this means I am short $5 in my tithes, and I have to make it up. Remember, the tithe is the Lord's. I took the Lord's money and used it for another purpose.

If I want to stay in a position where my channels will continue to be open and God can bless me with the windows-of-heaven blessings, then I have to keep that channel free by making up the $5 plus the 20 percent penalty. Twenty percent of $5 is $1, so I would have to pay back $6.

That may not sound like an astronomical sum, but consider this. What if you make $10,000 a month, and you take the entire tithe? Ten percent of $10,000 is $1,000. Twenty percent of $1,000 is $200. Instead of paying $1,000, you now have to pay $1,200 to keep your channel free. And that is just for one month. Can you imagine having to pay back three months' tithe at that rate? Or six months'? Or a year? The figures can add up quickly.

I think you would agree that it is much more reasonable to pay the tithe than it is to pay the penalty.

Someone may ask, "But what if I do not remember how much tithe money I took?" You may have to ask God to bring the figure to your remembrance. The fact God put a penalty into the system implies that you have to remember what you took from the Lord, so you will know you are operating based on that penalty, and redeem yourself out of the snare of the devil by straightening out your financial account with God.

Remember, the penalty is for those who have known about the mechanics of tithing, known the consequences of not paying their tithes, and have stopped paying them anyway. If you did not know before now about the things I have told you about, do not sweat it. You were operating in ignorance, and God will not hold you accountable for what you did not know. However, now that you know, you have a chance to start out "with a clean slate." I would urge you to get your act together with the Lord and to keep it together, because that is the best way to go.

Your Heavenly Bank Account

In the last chapter, we looked at Matthew 6:19-23, and talked about the fact that when Jesus told us not to lay up treasures on earth, but instead to lay up treasures in heaven, He was emphasizing that our hearts should be fixed on spiritual things first. Once our hearts are established in the right place, everything else will follow suit, including our finances.

One aspect we did not go over, but which we will discuss now is that Jesus tells us in those verses that we actually have a heavenly bank account.

Tithes and offerings are the way we make deposits into our heavenly bank account. If you do not make deposits, you cannot make withdrawals, and withdrawals from our heavenly bank account are how God meets our needs.

However, this also implies that if we make deposits, we can also make withdrawals. Here are five steps to remember and employ which will insure you receive your heavenly withdrawals.

1. Decide What You Want.

Be specific. James 1:7-8 says that you will not receive what you want if you are not specific, for the person who is not sure or wavers "is a double-minded man, unstable in all his ways."

2. Lay Hold on It by Faith.

Mark 11:23-24 tells us how we are to exercise our faith.

> "For assuredly, I say to you, whoever says to this mountain, 'Be removed and be cast into the sea,' and does not doubt in his heart, but believes that those things he says will be done, he will have whatever he says.
>
> "Therefore I say to you, whatever things you ask when you pray, believe that you receive them, and you will have them."

Decide what you want, be specific about it, then lay hold of it by faith, saying, "I believe that I receive."

Any two Believers can also do this by agreeing together according to Matthew 18:19:

Beware! The Lies of Satan

"Again I say to you that if two of you agree on earth concerning anything that they ask, it will be done for them by My Father in heaven."

If you are married, here is an area where you can agree with your spouse. You may not agree on the cat or the dog, or on the kind of food you are going to eat, but you can agree on the things of God. My wife and I did this, and we paid off a 30-year mortgage on our house in three years. Praise God!

3. Bind Satan's Power Over What Is Yours.

We have already covered this when we discussed Malachi 3:11. Jesus tells us in Mark 16:17, **"And these signs will follow those who believe: In My name they will cast out demons...."** James 4:7 says, **Therefore submit to God. Resist the devil, and he will flee from you.** When you pray, say, "Satan, in Jesus' name, I bind your power over what is mine. Take your hands off!" Then by faith see him obeying your command.

4. Loose the Forces of Heaven.

Hebrews 1:14 and Psalm 103:20 tell us about the angels. You have angels that are ministering spirits, sent forth to minister for you, just like waiters who are waiting a table in a restaurant. You tell those angels in prayer, in the name of Jesus, to go out and act on your behalf.

5. Praise God for the Answer.

Never forget to praise Him, in prayer, for the answer. Declare, say, and speak as though it were already done, because as far as God is concerned, it is an accomplished fact.

168

Jesus tells us in the first part of Luke 6:38, "Give, and it will be given to you: good measure, pressed down, shaken together, and running over will be put into your bosom...." Men will be the ones who will give it to you. God will be speaking to those men, but the blessings will come through the hands of men.

Keep in mind, though, that your incoming is based on your outgoing. If you do not like the incoming, you should change the outgoing, because Jesus says in the latter part of the same verse, "For [or because] with the same measure that you use, it will be measured back to you." Not a similar measure, but "the same measure." You are the one who controls what is going out. If you do not like what is coming back, you are the one who will have to change what is going out.

Let me say this, however, even though I emphasized it already. If you owe bills for which you have already made contractual arrangements, pay those bills first. I do not care how much you may want to tithe. Do not take money that belongs to your car payment, or your house payment, or other payments and tithe with it. That is not the way to do it.

God knows that you may have just found out about tithing, and that you may be up to your neck in debt. He knows you may not be able to tithe without letting your bills go, so do not wreck your testimony. Get the bills paid first. It may take some time, but God will honor you for your intention to give. Just honor that commitment when you can afford to tithe.

God has made a method available for us to free ourselves from financial circumstances, and we should be willing to take advantage of it. That method is through tithes and offerings. At the same time, we should not "give to get." We should tithe because we love the Lord and want to honor His Word. That should always be our motivation. If you "give to get," tithing will never work for you, because your motive is wrong, and God will not honor it. Give out of love, put your trust in the Lord to honor His Word and stand by faith on that Word continually. Then you will see a difference in your situation, and freedom will be yours.

Lie 10
You Do Not Love Me
If You Do Not Worry About Me

Most Christians worry all the time. They think they are supposed to worry about the husband, the wife, the kids, the job, the dog, the cat, and the goldfish, and that it is normal to do so. There are even people — Christians — who would prefer that you worry about them than for you to lay hands on them and say, "Be healed in Jesus' name," and then walk off. To them, when you sit around, worry and cry, it means you really care about them, even though it does not improve their circumstances one bit.

None of these people would ever think of worry as a sin. Perhaps you would not also, if you did not know what the Word of God says about it. But according to the Word of God, we are not supposed to worry or have fear about anything.

Worry is unbelief. It is a lack of faith. The Bible says that anything not of faith is sin, and worry is the worst sin you can commit. When you worry, you are telling God, "I cannot trust you to take care of this for me." If you cannot trust God to do something for you, you are in sad shape.

Let me put it another way. If you are trusting God, what are you worrying about?

It may seem oversimplified, but it is amazing how many people really do not take this attitude to heart. They say, "Of course, I trust God," and five minutes later they are back to worrying about this, that and the other thing. You have to have the attitude that whatever you would want to worry about is in God's hands, and be ready to stand on it no matter what comes up, if you are going to trust God and act like His Word is true.

Paul tells us in the first part of Philippians 4:6:

Be anxious for nothing....

The original Greek bears out this idea: Be not anxious to distraction. What it is saying here is to not be anxious to the point of distraction for anything, or about anything. In other words, do not let anything so occupy your time and your thinking that you become distracted from following after the Word of God.

If you think about it, and be honest about it, you can relate to what Paul is saying here. Some of us can relate to it in present tense. Others, like myself, can think about it in retrospect. I used to be a world champion worrier, and I was anxious about everything. I did not pray, because you cannot worry and pray at the same time. You cannot worry and study the Bible at the same time. So I was spending my time worrying, frustrated, uptight, bent out of shape, and nothing was being accomplished. I was just going down deeper and deeper into the quagmire.

Being trapped in worry is like being trapped in quicksand. If you relax and go limp, you will not go down so fast, and maybe someone can get to you and rescue you. But the more you struggle, the more it will suck you right in. That is what being anxious about things will do to you.

When you are worrying, you are not believing. When you are worrying, you are not exercising your faith. There is no way that you can worry and exercise your faith. One will cancel out the other. If you are worrying, you have canceled out faith. If you are operating in faith, you have canceled out worry.

Let me point out something else that is extremely important, because I come across this so much as a pastor in ministering to and counseling people. Paul tells us, "Be anxious for nothing." When Paul says, "... for nothing," he means for nothing. That includes your husband, your wife, your children, your job, your education, your pastorate, your people, your ministry, your money, your house, your car, your dog, the frog, and the hog. Paul says, "Be careful for nothing," so you cannot be careful for anything that has to do with your life.

How to Hand God Your Cares

A scripture that goes hand in hand with Philippians 4:6 is 1 Peter 5:7:

casting all your care upon Him, for He cares for you.

This verse and Philippians 4:6 say the same thing, but what 1 Peter 5:7 does is tell you how to do what Philippians 4:6 says. It is easy to say, "Be careful for nothing," but how do you go about doing it?

The way to be careful for nothing is by **casting all your care upon Him, for He cares for you.** *Cast* means to throw, so casting all your care upon the Lord means to throw it on Him.

Here is how you can cast your care on the Lord. Get a piece of paper, or more than one if you need it, and write down every care you have. When you are finished, go to the waste paper basket with that paper, and say the following:

"Lord, you told me in Your Word to cast all my care upon you. I cannot see You. I do not know where Your hand is, so if I threw my cares at You, I am not sure if I would be throwing them in the right direction. So, as an act of faith, I am going to say that this piece of paper, with all of these things listed on it, represent all of my cares and all of my concerns. This waste paper basket represents Your hand. I cast these cares upon You, Father, in the name of Jesus."

After you say that, ball up that paper, drop it in the waste paper basket, and leave it there. Once you leave it there you do not have it any more, and you are free.

If in fact you have cast your cares upon the Lord, you should ask yourself, "How does a free man think?" Once you answer that question, start thinking in line with the answer. Ask yourself, "How does a free man act," and start acting that way.

That is how you operate in faith. You may not feel any different psychologically, mentally, or physically, but we do not walk by feelings. We walk by faith. If you have cast your cares on the Lord, the Lord has them, and you do not. If you do not have them, you are free, so you have to start thinking free, talking free, and acting free. When you do that, it will cause the power of God to manifest in your circumstances to change them.

What many people want to do is feel like everything is better, and see that everything is better. Once they do that, they will believe that everything is better. That is foolish, because anything you see, you do not need to believe. When you see it, you should already know it. You only need to believe something, or exercise your faith, when you do not see it. Your faith takes the place of that thing until it arrives.

That is why Paul says in Hebrews 11:1 that faith is ... **the evidence of things not seen.** It is obvious from that statement that if you can see something, you do not need any faith, because faith is the evidence of things not seen. As long as I am not seeing the thing I am believing for, I have to use my faith, and faith takes the place of it until it arrives. Once it arrives, I do not need the evidence any longer, because I now have the thing for which I was believing. Therefore, I do not need to use my faith anymore, at least for that particular transaction of life.

I learned to cast all my cares on the Lord, and operate in faith that those cares are taken care of, many years ago. I have no cares — not one. There are certainly things I am interested in, things that I am concerned about in the sense that I want them to go right, but I do not worry about them. I have confessed the Word over them. I do my part to get things done. I go by faith that God is taking care of His part, and that He is well able to do it.

I do not even worry about people talking about me. I do not try to trace down the origin of a statement, or ask, "Who said that?" People can say what they want. What they say does not make it true. What I say is what makes it true. What they say is merely opinion. What I say is putting faith into operation. So what I think and say about myself, and what I do, is what makes me who I am, not what people may say. I would like everything that is said about me to be nice, but if some of those things are not positive, guess what? I could care less.

I cannot afford to care about things like that. If I did care, I would be in violation of my Father's Word, because He told me, **casting all your care upon Him, for He cares for you.** Those people are my care. Those people are the ones I am concerned about, but they do not belong to me. They belong to Jesus. He redeemed them, purchased them, through what He did for them. I did not. He is the one making intercession for them in heaven, and He is the one coming for them at the end of the age. So I have cast my cares about them, as well as everything else, on Him.

That does not mean I do not have the opportunity to care about some things. But I found out that having those cares is not profitable. It does not pay to carry them, so I stopped doing it. When I found out how to be free in the Word, I decided to take full advantage of it — and you should make it a point to do the same.

By Prayer, With Thanksgiving

Let us go back to Philippians 4:6, and notice something else.

> Be anxious for nothing, but in everything by prayer and supplication, with thanksgiving, let your requests be made known to God.

What Paul is telling us to do here is to take those things we would be concerned about, and make a request to God concerning them. If your husband is your concern, you should make a request to God concerning your husband. If it is your job, make a request to God about it.

He goes on to say that we should make those requests **with thanksgiving.** What are we thanking God for? Are we thanking God that we have a problem? No. We are thanking God that we believe we have the answer to the desires of our heart. We have exercised our faith, so we are thanking God that we have somebody who will work on our behalf — Almighty God.

We have God on our side, so we should put God on those concerns. You know how somebody has a dog, and they turn it loose and say, "Sick 'em," when they want to get rid of something or somebody? That is what we should do with our cares. We should tell God, "Sick 'em!" That way, you can keep prospering. You can sleep good at night, with a clear conscience, and keep the channels of faith open for God to take care of you.

Paul says, **Be anxious for nothing, but in everything by prayer and supplication,...** so you had better learn how to pray. Did you notice that Paul does not say anything here about praying hard? He says, **... but in everything by prayer and supplication, with thanksgiving, let your requests be made known to God.**

The word *requests* is plural. Thank God for that. That means you can go to God with anything in your life. You can go to Him 9,000,000 times, if you need to, for 9,000,000 different commodities. Whatever it is, He will take care of it when you bring it to Him. Learn to cast it upon Him. The way you do that is through prayer. That is the medium of exchange here.

I was talking with a woman one time, and certain things were mentioned in the course of the conversation. So I said to her, "Why don't you ask the Lord to do something?" She replied, "I don't want to ask the Lord for too much. He has already done so much."

That is an attitude that Christians sometimes get into — that the Lord has already done so much that they do not want to wear out their welcome. You cannot do that. Remember this: If the Lord did not want to be bothered with you, He would have never told you to come boldly to the throne. After all, doesn't God know human nature? Doesn't He know that we will wear Him out by coming for every little thing? Why would He say to cast all our cares upon Him if He did not want to be bothered?

God wants us free. If we cast our cares upon Him, He has them, and we do not. That leaves us free, because God knows how to handle it.

Man Is Not Made for Worry

You are not built for worry. You are not built for cares. So when you worry or care, it destroys you physically and mentally. It will open the door for disease, sickness, and malfunctioning organs in your body. Worry is more deadly than cancer. We may not think so, because

99 times out of 100, when we hear about someone with cancer, the person we hear about ends up dying. Consequently, we do not see many cases where the doctor certifies that a person has died from worry. But if you look closely at many of the cases of cancer, heart disease, and nervous breakdowns (not to mention many other things), you will find that worry was the chief ingredient that precipitated the demise of the individual.

Man is not made for worry. You do not have overload circuits built into you. What happens is that when you worry, you destroy what is already there in your body. You may not realize this, because there are usually no immediate physical effects from worry that we are aware of. But when you continue to worry and do not walk in faith, the physical and mental effects accumulate over time.

That is also why many people do not have their prayers answered. They are saying all the right words, but they are worrying. When you worry, you cancel out your prayer, because you cannot worry and trust at the same time. You do one or the other.

Here is how you know when you are worrying. If you are worrying about something, you are always thinking about it. If it is always in your mind, you are worrying about it. If you have cast the problem on the Lord, and you do not have it, why would it be on your mind? The only thing that would be there if you cast the problem on the Lord would be when you prayed, "Lord, thank you that my husband is saved," or "Thank you that my child is doing right." You would not sit there all day long thinking about the challenge you may be having with your husband or child. You would not wring your hands over the situation or be frustrated about it.

If you are worrying, I have news for you. As long as you have your little hot hands on the situation, the Lord will not touch it. He will stand there and watch you go down the tubes, because He cannot touch the problem until you turn it loose. That is the way He has designed the system.

Imagine a jar that has a lid open just far enough for you to slip your hand through. In fact, you have to force your hand in. If you pick up a coin inside that jar, and put your fist around it, you will never get your hand out. You have to let go of that coin to get your hand out.

That is the way it is with the issues of life. As long as you have your hand involved, God will not touch those things that are bugging you, so you have to turn them over to Him. The thing that is so sad about this is that you can think you have turned the situation over to God, but you are still worrying about it, and because of that, He is not going to get involved.

Stop worrying. "But Brother Price, you just don't understand." I do not have to. It is not I who told you to stop — it is your Father. And if you tell me that He does not know what you are going through, you are truly deceived. He is the one who said, *Be anxious for nothing.* That implies it is possible not to be anxious.

I used to think when I was caught up with worrying that I could not survive without it. I had myself convinced that I had to worry, that if I did not do so, nothing would be done about my situation. Worrying was a part of everyday life. After all, how do you live without worrying?

I will tell you how — free! It is easy. And once you decide to live a free life, you will never go back to worrying again.

Notice, I said that *you decide* to live a free life. You are the only one who can deliver yourself from worry. It would be great if you could pray and say, "Cast this thing out of me, Brother Price," and I could say, "Come out of this person, in Jesus' name." But it does not work that way. When God says, **Be anxious for nothing,** He is telling us to do just that. When He says, **casting all your care upon Him,** He is telling you to cast your cares on Him. That is your responsibility. If you do not do it, it will not be done. So learn to trust, and not to worry.

The Peace of God

Philippians 4:6-7:

Be anxious for nothing, but in everything by prayer and supplication, with thanksgiving, let your requests be made known to God;
and the peace of God, which surpasses all understanding, will guard your hearts and minds through Christ Jesus.

The peace of God will keep your heart and mind free of anything that would entangle them or hold them in bondage. But notice, the peace of God, which passes all understanding, does not come into operation until you are anxious for nothing, and have by prayer and supplication with thanksgiving made your requests known to God. The peace of God will not keep you until you do those things.

There are many people who are restless and not at peace. They are in turmoil spiritually and mentally. It is the saddest thing to see, especially when you know they do not have to be that way.

Once you are not anxious for anything and have cast your cares on the Lord, you will be at peace, because you will be free from every concern. That is a good way to measure whether or not you have actually cast your cares upon the Lord. If you do not have peace about something, it means you still have it.

Understanding in verse seven means human understanding. Proverbs 3:5 tells us, **Trust in the Lord with all your heart, and lean not on your own understanding.** When you try using your natural, human understanding, you will be inclined to think, "How can I live without worrying about my husband," or "How can I live without worrying about my wife? I can't do it!"

Your human understanding cannot comprehend what God is saying here. Until I found out how to operate in the peace of God, I felt as though I could not pay the bills without worrying about them first. But the peace of God passes all understanding, and the good thing about it is that you do not have to *understand* it! All you have to do is enjoy God's peace.

When you think about it, there is really very little you have to understand in order to enjoy the benefits of having the peace of God. For instance, if you drop a match into a jar of gasoline, the gasoline will explode and blow that jar apart. However, when we drive an automobile, we are mixing gasoline and fire, and it does not blow the car's engine apart. Many of us do not understand why that does not happen, or even care. We just take advantage of the car's operation when we go driving somewhere.

Notice one other thing in verse seven. It says the peace of God **will guard your hearts and minds through Christ Jesus.** Because *hearts* and *minds* are mentioned as two separate things, it is obvious that your heart and your mind are not the same. If they were the same, this verse would say either "shall keep your heart" or "shall keep your mind." It would not say **hearts and minds.**

As I have said many times, your heart is your spirit. It is the real you. You are a spirit, you have a soul, and you live in a physical body. Your mind is located in the soul realm, or the soul part of you. God says that He will keep your heart and your mind. If God is keeping His peace in your heart and mind, then because you are at peace, it will allow your heart and your mind to exert an influence over your body, and keep your body in line without any problem whatsoever. When you find someone whose body is not functioning correctly, you probably have a person who does not have peace in his heart and mind, and he is in confusion.

Think About These

Philippians 4:8:

Finally, brethren, whatever things are true, whatever things are noble, whatever things are

just, whatever things are pure, whatever things are lovely, whatever things are of good report, if there is any virtue and if there is anything praiseworthy — meditate on these things.

Here is what you should think about — not on what calamities can befall your family or your job, because those things are not pure, lovely, or of good report. You should confess that the angels of the Lord are encamped around your family, that whatsoever you put your hands to shall prosper, including your job, and that nothing you put your hands to shall fail. Those are the things you should think on, as well as all the other blessings God promises you in His Word.

Understand that this is not thought control. God is not trying to control your thoughts. He is showing you a principle by which you can operate in and enjoy the peace of God. The way you do that is to think on the things mentioned in Philippians 4:8. When you are thinking on whatever is true, noble, honest, just, pure, lovely and of good report, you do not have time to think about worrying. Remember also that faith comes by hearing, and hearing by the Word of God. The more you confess what God promises you, the more faith you will have for it, and the more you will operate in this principle — as well as having what you say come to pass.

This is going to require a value judgment on your part. You will have to make an evaluation on everything that comes to you. You will have to determine whether it is true, noble, just, pure, lovely and of good report. It may be true that the preacher ran away with the organist, but it is not lovely, or of good report, so you should not think about it.

All of these ingredients have to be involved for you to think on something. It is not just thinking on something that is true. It is not just thinking on something that is just, or something that is lovely. What you have to think on has to be true, noble, just, pure, lovely, of good report, have virtue, and have praise. That is covering a lot of bases.

If Christians really did this — and it is sad how few Christians really do it — then gossip, among other things, would cease instantly. Gossip is usually not just, or lovely, or of good report. It is not just to talk about someone when you do not have all the facts, and with gossip, you do not have the facts. You usually have partial, distorted, embellished knowledge, so it is certainly not good to talk about, let alone think about.

You have to watch your mouth. You have to really be careful when you talk about someone. There will be times when you have to talk about someone, and by that, I mean that you will have to mention a person's name, and make some statements about that person. But you need to be careful that you are not being judgmental, and that you do not get the idea that what you heard someone else say about a person is automatically true.

When someone tries to tell me about someone or something, I always say, "Maybe that's not true." And many times, it is really not true. Sometimes, you have a situation in which someone was supposed to do something, and did not do it. It is tempting to go into a rage, and say, "Why didn't that person do this," but there may have been some extenuating circumstances, something beyond the person's control, that prevented him from doing it. Many times, you find out that is exactly the case. You need to be very careful about all these things, because they will have an impact on your faith and on your life.

Does It Have Virtue?

Paul says in the latter part of Philippians 4:8, ... **if there is any virtue and if there is anything praiseworthy — meditate on these things.** *Virtue* means "moral goodness." If you have virtue and praise present in what you hear about something, not to mention all the other things mentioned in that verse, then go ahead and think on what you heard, and praise God for it.

If you took what Paul says here seriously, you would not think about many of the things people do, what they say, or how they act, because they are not honest, lovely, just, or any of the other things on this list. Paul tells us what to think on, then says, ... **think on these things.** Whose responsibility is it to think on these things? Just as when you stop worrying and trust God, the responsibility is yours.

When you decide to **think on these things,** you will have to adjust your thinking. While you are doing this, you will be challenged. Satan will assault you constantly with thoughts that have no virtue or praise about them, but you do not have to think about them. That, again, is your choice.

Your mind is open to Satan, and it is open to God. Satan cannot read your mind. If he could read your mind, he would know what you were going to do, and he could block you at every step. Especially if it were something you were going to do for God, wouldn't Satan try to block it? Think about how many things you have gotten away with doing for God, that Satan did not block you from doing. That should prove he cannot read your mind.

The only way Satan knows what you are thinking is when he suggests a thought to you, and you pick up that thought and start talking about it. Satan is not God. Many times, people have thought that Satan had the same abilities as God, but because Satan is God's enemy does not mean he is God's equal. Far from it. Satan is not even equal to one of God's angels. As we mentioned in the first chapter, Satan is really an angel, but he is a fallen angel, and he has no anointing. Therefore, he is not even on the same level as Gabriel, Michael, or any other archangel.

Satan cannot make you do anything, and he cannot read your mind. All he can do is influence you by suggestion. But the Bible says that you can just as easily dismiss that thought and concentrate instead on the Word.

2 Corinthians 10:1-5:

Now I, Paul, myself am pleading with you by the meekness and gentleness of Christ — who in presence am lowly among you, but being absent am bold toward you.

But I beg you that when I am present I may not be bold with that confidence by which I intend to be bold against some, who think of us as if we walked according to the flesh.

> For though we walk in the flesh, we do not war according to the flesh.
>
> For the weapons of our warfare are not carnal but mighty through God for pulling down strongholds,
>
> casting down arguments and every high thing that exalts itself against the knowledge of God, bringing every thought into captivity to the obedience of Christ.

Arguments in verse five is literally the word *reasonings,* and God tells us to cast them down — in other words, to throw them away. That is fine, but how do you know when something exalts itself against the knowledge of God?

The only way you can know that, and the only way you can bring anything into the obedience of Christ, is by having an accurate knowledge of the Word. You have to measure everything by the Word, to determine whether or not it exalts itself against the knowledge of God, because the knowledge of God is revealed in the Word of God. You should submit every thought that comes into your mind to the Word. Whatever that thought is, find out what the Word says about it, and see whether or not it measures up. If it measures up, you can think about it. If it does not, throw it down, and bring every thought into the obedience of Christ.

Again, the obedience of Christ is also the Word of God. Christ has already told you what He wants you to do in His Word, so all you have to do to be obedient to Christ is to be obedient to the Word. The Bible says in 2 Timothy 2:15, **Be diligent [the King James Bible says to study] to present yourself approved to God, a workman who does not need to be ashamed, rightly dividing**

the word of truth. Study and do what God says to do in His Word, continue to cast your cares upon the Lord, and you will have it "made in the shade."

Lie 11
Speaking With Tongues Is of the Devil

1 John 4:1-4:

> Beloved, do not believe every spirit, but test the spirits, whether they are of God; because many false prophets have gone out into the world.
>
> By this you know the Spirit of God: Every spirit that confesses Jesus Christ has come in the flesh is of God,
>
> and every spirit that does not confess that Jesus Christ has come in the flesh is not of God. And this is the spirit of the Antichrist, which you have heard was coming, and is now already in the world.
>
> You are of God, little children, and have overcome them, because He who is in you is greater than he who is in the world.

He who is in the world refers to the evil spirits, the forces of Satan, that are running loose in this world. Even though we have the victory over them through Christ Jesus, we still have to contend with them on an everyday basis.

The Greater One, or **He who is in you,** is the Spirit of God. Jesus is in us, of course, **Christ in you, the hope of glory,** but the way He is in us is by the Holy Spirit. Through the Holy Spirit, the power of God is made available to us, and that power is our ultimate weapon to use against these demon forces.

This does not in any way negate or water down the importance of faith. You need to know how to operate in faith and how to release your faith on whatever may arise. That is extremely important. However, if you do not release any power on a situation when you try to use your faith, you still do not have anything. We need a combination of faith and power, because they both work together.

You have to be filled with the Holy Spirit to have that power available to you. Otherwise, you will not overcome those who are in the world. And those demon forces are ready to shoot you down at every turn.

The only way you can combat these forces is by the power of God. The Holy Spirit is the power, and speaking with tongues is the "valve" that releases that power.

Satan wants you powerless, so he can control and dominate you. That is one reason he tenaciously fights speaking with tongues, and one reason why you should participate in it. The devil has even ascended to some pulpits, and said through the mouths of those who are supposed to be representing God, "Speaking with tongues is of the devil. Watch out for that."

Do you notice how inconsistent this statement really is? In every other lie of Satan mentioned in this book, there is no such thing as the devil. God is supposed to be the one who brings bad things on people, because, by the process of elimination, God is the only spiritual entity left after you discount Satan. After all, you cannot blame some calamity on someone who does not exist, right?

Either the devil exists, or he does not; you cannot have it both ways. And as we read in chapter one, the devil does exist. He is a thief, a murderer, and many other sordid and unpleasant things, and he will do anything — I repeat, anything — to keep you ignorant, so he can keep messing over you.

When it comes to speaking with tongues, the fact of the matter, plain and simple, is this: Without the power released by speaking with tongues, we are pushovers for the devil. You have to have that supernatural ability. Satan knows this, and he will lie to you and try to scare you away from tongues at all costs.

Satan's strategy is this: His first step is to keep you from coming to Christ. If you come to Christ, his next step is to keep you ignorant of the power available to you. If that does not work, Satan's third step is to try to scare you off. He will put thoughts into your mind like, "Well, you know you do not want to be different," or "Speaking with tongues is what those holy rollers do — you know, the ones who do not wear any make-up, wear funny clothes, and roll down the aisles every chance they get."

The thing is, some of the people who say those things have never seen anyone roll down an aisle in their lives! What is a "holy roller"? What does a holy roller look like that an unholy roller does not look like? They never read it in the Bible, but they got it off the street or from some place that calls itself a church.

Two Separate Transactions

Another idea which has prevailed in several denominations is that when you are born again, you are automatically filled with the spirit, as well. This was true in the first church my wife and I attended after I was saved. This church taught that getting saved and being filled with the Spirit were the same thing. Notice an incident which occurs in the 19th chapter of Acts, however.

Acts 19:1-2:

> And it happened, while Apollos was at Corinth, that Paul, having passed through the upper regions, came to Ephesus. And finding some disciples
> he said to them, "Did you receive the Holy Spirit when you believed?"...

Remember that the events in Acts 19 happened approximately 19 years after the day of Pentecost. The Church had been operating in the power of the Spirit for those 19 years. Paul at this time had been ministering the Gospel by the leading and the power of the Holy Spirit for about nine or ten years, so he definitely knew what he was doing by this time.

Acts 19:2-6:

> he said to them, "Did you receive the Holy Spirit when you believed?" So they said to him, "We have not so much as heard whether there is a Holy Spirit."
> And he said to them, "Into what then were you baptized?" So they said, "Into John's baptism."
> Then Paul said, "John indeed baptized with the baptism of repentance, saying to the people that they should believe on Him who would come after him, that is, on Christ Jesus."

When they heard this, they were baptized in the name of the Lord Jesus.

And when Paul had laid hands on them, the Holy Spirit came upon them, and they spoke with tongues and prophesied.

If what they told me in that church was true, why did Paul ask the people in Ephesus, **"Did you receive the Holy Spirit when you believed?"** His asking that question implies that being filled with the Spirit is not automatic.

Also, Jesus says in John 14:17 that *the world* — sinners — cannot receive the Holy Spirit. If you are filled with the Spirit at the same moment you are born again, you are receiving Him while you are a sinner. Jesus says you cannot do that. You can accept Jesus as your personal Lord and Savior at 12:00, then be filled with the Spirit at 12:01, but you cannot do both things simultaneously.

Being born again and being filled with the Spirit are two separate transactions. The Holy Spirit is in you only if you receive Him by an act of your will, after you have been born again. It may not be theologically or denominationally true, but it is biblically true.

There are many people who think being filled with the Spirit is good, fine, and wonderful. Some of them even say that they should be filled, and would, except that they do not want to speak with other tongues. That one aspect of being filled with the Spirit repels them.

God will not force you to be filled with the Spirit, just as He will not force you to be born again. It is entirely your decision. However, if you decide you do not need to be filled, you should amass enough evidence from the Word to be able to tell God why you do not have to be filled with His Holy Spirit. I do not mean basing your case on one solitary verse of scripture. Find several, because the Bible tells us, **By the mouth of two or three witnesses every word shall be established.**

The Case For Tongues

How did the apostles know when someone was filled with the Spirit? We have ways in many industries of determining whether a product is genuine or counterfeit, so more than likely, the apostles had some method, also. What was the norm or benchmark they used?

Usually, if you want to establish a norm for something, you go back to the first time that event occurred and establish your norm based on that. We will look at the first time people were filled with the Holy Spirit and see what happened. Then we will look at other scriptures to find out if the apostles used what happened that first time as a benchmark.

In Acts 2:1-4, we have the first occurrence of people being filled with the Spirit:

> **When the Day of Pentecost had fully come, they were all with one accord in one place.**
> **And suddenly there came a sound from heaven, as of a rushing mighty wind, and it filled the whole house where they were sitting.**

> Then there appeared to them divided tongues, as of fire, and one sat upon each of them.
> And they were all filled with the Holy Spirit and began to speak with other tongues, as the Spirit gave them utterance.

Notice the connection here: **And they were all filled with the Holy Spirit and began to speak with other tongues.** It does not say, "And they were all filled with the Holy spirit," period. It says they were filled with the Holy Spirit and began to speak with other tongues, as the Spirit gave them utterance.

We have the same connection emphasized in Acts 10:44-46:

> While Peter was still speaking these words, the Holy Spirit fell upon all those who heard the word.
> And those of the circumcision who believed were astonished, as many as came with Peter, because the gift of the Holy Spirit had been poured out on the Gentiles also.
> For they heard them speak with tongues and magnify God....

In Acts 19:6, the same thing happened when the people in Ephesus received the Holy Spirit.

> And when Paul had laid hands on them, the Holy Spirit came upon them, and they spoke with tongues and prophesied.

Every time someone in the book of Acts was filled with the Spirit, it was accompanied by speaking with other tongues. I submit to you that speaking with tongues was the benchmark the apostles used to determine if someone had been filled with the Spirit.

Go back to Acts 10:27-28, and I will prove that what I have just stated is the case.

> **And as he talked with him** [this is Peter talking with a man named Cornelius], **he** [Peter] **went in and found many who had come together.**
> **Then he** [Peter] **said to them, "You know how unlawful it is for a Jewish man to keep company with or go to one of another nation. But God has shown me that I should not call any man common or unclean."**

The context of these verses is this: Peter was an Orthodox Jew. Because of a vision the Lord gave him, he went to the home of a man named Cornelius. Cornelius was a Gentile, and at this point in time, most Orthodox Jews would have frowned upon Peter's going to the home of a Gentile.

Acts 10:44-11:15:

> **While Peter was still speaking these words, the Holy Spirit fell upon all those who had heard the word.**
> **And those of the circumcision** [that is, the Jews] **who believed were astonished, as many as came with Peter, because the gift of the Holy Spirit had been poured out on the Gentiles also.**

For they heard them speak with tongues and magnify God. Then Peter answered, "Can anyone forbid water, that these should not be baptized, who have received the Holy Spirit just as we have?"

And he commanded them to be baptized in the name of the Lord. Then they asked him to stay a few days.

Now the apostles and brethren who were in Judea heard that the Gentiles had also received the word of God.

And when Peter came up to Jerusalem, those of the circumcision [the Jews] contended with him,

saying, "You went in to uncircumcised men and ate with them!"

But Peter explained it to them in order from the beginning, saying:

"I was in the city of Joppa praying; and in a trance I saw a vision, an object descending like a great sheet, let down from heaven by four corners; and it came to me.

"When I observed it intently and considered, I saw four-footed animals of the earth, wild beasts, creeping things, and birds of the air.

"And I heard a voice saying to me, 'Rise, Peter; kill and eat.'

"But I said, 'Not so, Lord! For nothing common or unclean has at any time entered my mouth.'

"But the voice answered me again from heaven, 'What God has cleansed you must not call common.'

"Now this was done three times, and all were drawn up again into heaven.

"At that very moment, three men stood before the house where I was, having been sent from Caesarea.

"Then the Spirit told me to go with them, doubting nothing. Moreover these six brethren accompanied me, and we entered the man's house.

"And he told us how he had seen an angel standing in his house, who said to him, 'Send men to Joppa, and call for Simon, whose surname is Peter,

"who will tell you words by which you and all
your household will be saved.'
"And as I began to speak, the Holy Spirit fell
upon them, as upon us...."

Fell upon them, as upon us. In more modern terms,
we would say, "Fell on them like He fell on us." Now pay
close attention to what Peter says in the rest of this verse.

"And as I began to speak, the Holy Spirit fell
upon them, as upon us at the beginning."

Peter reminded the Jews who were contending
with him of what happened to them when they were
filled. He went back to the beginning. We can deduce
from Peter's statement that what happened in the
beginning was the apostles' benchmark, and that it
should be our benchmark, as well. Not the beginning
as in your denomination's beginning, not back to the
seminary, but where the Word indicates it started.

Acts 11:16-18:

"Then I remembered the word of the Lord, how
He said, 'John indeed baptized with water, but you
shall be baptized with the Holy Spirit.'
"If therefore God gave them the same gift as He
gave us when we believed on the Lord Jesus Christ,
who was I that I could withstand God?"
When they [the Jews] heard these things. they
became silent; and they glorified God, saying, "Then
God has also granted to the Gentiles repentance to life."

200

Convincing the Jews to fellowship with the Gentiles was a monumental happening, because they were not the kind of people who accepted every whimsical idea. It took God Almighty the spiritual equivalent of an atomic bomb to get them to change what they were believing, because they were so thoroughly entrenched in what they believed. I do not mean anything derogatory by saying that, but I simply mention it to prove my point.

The point is, if what happened in those verses was enough to convince these Jews, it should be enough to convince us.

Why Speak?

The question we have to ask ourselves, inevitably, is, Why speak with tongues? In other words, why do tongues come with the package of being filled with the Holy Spirit? One reason we have already discussed is that speaking with tongues releases the power of God into your life and circumstances. But that is only one reason. What are some others?

We read in Acts 10:45, **And those of the circumcision who believed were astonished, as many as came with Peter, because the gift of the Holy Spirit had been poured out on the Gentiles also.** The Holy Spirit, like salvation, is a gift. We do nothing to earn it or be worthy of it. We simply accept it. When you receive a gift, or when a gift is offered to you, you do not dictate the terms of what is being offered. The giver does. You have only two options. You can either accept it, or reject it.

Let me give you an example of what I mean. Let us say someone wants to bless you with a brand new car. You do not have to pay a cent for it, and there are no conditions or strings attached. All you have to do is drive the car, take care of it, and enjoy it. However, when the car is delivered to your house, you find out the car is red. You do not like the color red.

Is the fact the car is red going to stop you from accepting it? Probably not. A car is a car, and cars are not cheap. In fact, chances are that you will want to take it around the block for a spin right away.

God is the one who is giving us the car — the Holy Spirit — and He is the one who made it red by the speaking with other tongues.

Here is another reason for speaking with tongues. If you ask anyone whether or not that person would desire to speak to God, the answer you generally get will be yes. But we never stop to consider two things: how limited our native languages really are, and how limited our access to God is because of our lack of knowledge about persons, places, or things.

We can say in our native languages to the Father, "I want to thank you for this day. I want to thank you for your blessings. I want to thank you that I am your child, that through Jesus you have saved me, redeemed me, and written my name in the Lamb's Book of Life." However, we get to the point where we say, "I thank you, I thank you, I thank you," and we are not really saying what we want to say, but we know no other words in our native languages.

That is where speaking with tongues can be beneficial. Through it, we can converse with God beyond

202

the realm of our individual knowledge about the circumstances around us, and we can express to the Father everything we want to say to Him.

Another place where speaking with tongues can help is in the area of intercession. Paul says in Romans 8:26-27:

> Likewise the Spirit also helps in our weaknesses [or ability to understand and know]. **For we do not know what we should pray for as we ought, but the Spirit Himself makes intercession for us with groanings which cannot be uttered.**
> **Now He who searches the hearts knows what the mind of the Spirit is, because He makes intercession for the saints according to the will of God.**

Many times, people will look at this scripture and say, "You know, we don't know how to pray as we should." That is not what Paul is referring to here. I mentioned that one of the things that limits us in our speaking with God is our lack of knowledge about persons, places, and things. That is especially true in the case of intercession. It is not so much not knowing how to pray as it is not knowing how to "pray as we ought" — in other words, not knowing what to pray for.

For example, let us say that I want to pray and intercede for you. I do not know anything about your life — whether or not you are having any problems, if you are sick, what shape your finances are in. I cannot intelligently pray for your needs when I do not know what those needs are. Just praying, "Bless him, Lord" will not solve the problem either. There is no point in blessing you with physical healing blessings if you need money. If you are standing against cancer or some other life-threatening illness, you do not need a million dollars. You need divine healing.

I still want to pray for you, but what can I do? Simple. I can intercede on your behalf in the spirit, with other tongues, as the Holy Spirit gives me utterance. The Holy Spirit knows your needs, just are He knows everything else about you. That is what Paul is writing about in Romans 8:27.

In both praise and intercession, we can use speaking with tongues to converse with God. In 1 Corinthians 14:2, Paul says:

> For he who speaks in a tongue does not speak to men but to God, for no one understands him; however, in the spirit he speaks mysteries.

You may think, "But Pastor Price, how am I supposed to know what I am saying. If what Paul says is true, I won't understand a word I say when I speak with tongues." That is correct. If **no one understands him** when a person speaks with tongues, that means the person speaking cannot understand it, either. But I want you to read this verse one more time, and notice something very important.

> For he who speaks in a tongue does not speak to men, but to God, for no one understands him; however, in the spirit he speaks mysteries.

Notice, the word *spirit* is in small case, as it ought to be. It indicates we are speaking out of our spirits when we speak in tongues to God.

Hebrews 12:9 tells us that God is **the Father of spirits.** We have been brought into right relationship with God, so God is the Father of our recreated human spirits — the real us. God wants you to talk to Him in a language no one can mess with, and He loves each one of us so much that He has given us a private means of communication with Him. No one can eavesdrop on us. No one can jam the frequency. Not even our intellectual minds can get in the way, because this ability transcends the human intellect, and everything else man can come up with. You have a straight line — a hot line — directly to the throne of God.

When we speak with tongues to the Father, the devil cannot tap the line. That is one reason he fights tongues so tenaciously. When you converse in your native language, the devil can monitor what you say. He can make insidious suggestions and infiltrate your mind with other thoughts while you are talking to God. But when you speak with tongues, God has locked the devil out, and that infuriates Satan.

Speaking With Tongues and the Gift of Tongues

Let me make a distinction here between speaking with tongues and the gift of tongues, which is actually one of the nine "gifts of the Spirit" mentioned in 1 Corinthians 12. Speaking with tongues is for every Christian. However, the gift of tongues is not for every Christian, just as not every Christian will be used with the gifts of healings or the gift of working of miracles.

The gift of tongues is something entirely different from speaking with tongues, and it operates as the Spirit wills, not as we will.

The gift of tongues is for public assembly, and 99 times out of 100, it is accompanied by the companion gift of the interpretation of tongues. Speaking with tongues, on the other hand, is for your personal spiritual worship and praise, and for your own spiritual contact with God. It is for your spiritual enrichment. It does not need an interpretation, because it is between you and God.

Here is an easy way to remember the difference. Speaking with tongues is man talking to God; it goes from earth to heaven. The gift of tongues goes from heaven to earth, because it is God speaking through a man to other men.

At a meeting in Oklahoma, I had just finished ministering the Word, and was led by the Spirit into the manifestation of the gift of tongues. I spoke a word to the congregation, then gave the interpretation. We went on, everyone rejoiced and praised the Lord, as the word the Spirit spoke through me was edifying, encouraging and inspiring.

After the meeting, a young man came to share something with me. He mentioned that his wife was fluent in seven languages, then asked me if I knew what I was saying when I spoke in tongues to the congregation. I said that I did not, but that I believed it was the leading of the Spirit of God. He then told me that his wife said I was speaking perfect Portuguese, and that the interpretation I gave was totally accurate.

There is no way in the natural that I can speak fluent Portuguese. In the natural, I know just one phrase of that language, and the only reason I know that much is that while I was with the Presbyterian church, we had a pastor from Brazil who stayed with us, and he taught a class in Portuguese. But in the Spirit, I gave a whole message in that language. That was something supernatural. And it blessed the people.

Something else that occasionally confuses people is when they hear someone speak with tongues for two minutes, then hear another person speak in his native language for only 30 seconds to give the interpretation. Right away, they think, "That can't be from God."

What those people are doing is confusing the word *interpretation* with the word *translation*. A translation of something is a word-for-word definition of what was said. An interpretation is simply the summary of what was said.

Imagine this scene: One day, as I was jogging through the countryside, I came upon a meadow. As I was jogging past the meadow, I heard the sound of rustling in the bushes to my right. I saw a rabbit emerge from the thickets, and cross the path in front of me. It went over a little hill, down a ravine, and up the side of a mountain. Then I heard another sound, and close behind the rabbit was a dog. The dog also crossed the road in front of me, went down the ravine into the valley, and up the mountainside. I could hear the baying of the dog as he pursued the rabbit.

That is the complete scenario. The interpretation of that scene is, the dog chased the rabbit. That was the gist of the story; the rest was simply embellishment. The gift of interpretation of tongues works the same way.

Charging Your Spiritual Batteries

First Corinthians 14:4 tells us:

He who speaks in a tongue edifies himself, but he who prophesies edifies the church.

Sometimes the church needs to be edified. That is when the "vocal gifts" of the Spirit go into operation in the corporate Body — either the gift of prophecy, or the gift of divers tongues with the companion gift of interpretation of tongues. However, there are also times when we need to be edified, and God has provided a way by which we can do just that.

The word *edify* means "to build up." The best word in English to correspond to this is the word *charge*, as in charging a car battery when it is run down. Your spirit tires just like your body does and needs its energy replenished — especially if you are operating in spiritual things, and you are engaged in spiritual warfare with the powers of darkness. That warfare can tax you, so you need a way for your spirit to "charge its batteries."

The way you re-energize your spirit is by speaking with tongues. In fact, it is the only way you edify yourself when you pray, because the only time the Bible refers to doing that is in reference to speaking with other tongues.

If the devil can keep you in a state of spiritual exhaustion, he can whip up on you whenever he wants. But if he lets you recuperate, he knows he has a problem on his hands. That is why he keeps bombarding Christians with everything he can muster — especially when some of them find out how to be edified!

A verse which echoes what we just read in I Corinthians 14, and adds something else that is very important, is Jude 20. There Jude says:

> **But you, beloved, building yourselves up on your most holy faith, praying in the Holy Spirit.**

Praying in the Holy Spirit will not give you faith, because faith comes by hearing, and hearing by the Word of God. Praying in the Holy Spirit will build you up on your most holy faith. It will strengthen you — and you do it yourself.

You pray in the Holy Spirit by praying in the spirit, since it is the Holy Spirit who prompts your spirit and gives it the language so you can pray in the spirit. Or as Paul puts it in I Corinthians 14:14:

> **For if I pray in a tongue, my spirit prays....**

That means the opposite also has to be true — if I do not pray in a tongue, my spirit does not pray.

> **For if I pray in a tongue, my spirit prays, but my understanding is unfruitful.**

We can infer from what Paul says here that your spirit and your understanding are different. Now look at the next verse.

> **What is the conclusion then? I will pray with the spirit, and I will also pray with the understanding....**

The word *also* means "in addition to." It does not mean that you do both things at the same time, nor can you. It would be like trying to say "dog" in English and in another language at the same moment — and that is impossible. It means you should take the time to pray both ways — in the understanding first, then in the spirit, or vice verse.

I pray in my understanding — in my natural human ability, using my own language — because I may be praying about something specific, and I need to use my native language to describe that thing, explain it, and lay claim to it by faith. When I pray in the spirit, I build myself up, charging up my spiritual battery. We can do both those things, which are very advantageous for us.

> **What is the conclusion then? I will pray with the spirit, and I will also pray with the understanding. I will sing with the spirit, and I will also sing with the understanding.**

Some people who speak with tongues never sing in the spirit. You sing in the spirit the same way you talk in the spirit — you just open your mouth and begin. "But I do not know the song." You do not have to. You will get a melody, and go on from there.

It is beautiful when you sing in the spirit. There is a quality about it that is supernatural, especially if you get a group of people together who are all in agreement with it. Singing in the spirit ushers you into another realm and does something to you and for you.

"But I Don't Want to Get Too Holy"

Some people are afraid of being filled with the Holy Spirit because they do not want to live too holy a lifestyle. Do not worry. The Holy Spirit will not make you do anything you do not want to do. You can keep on fornicating, if you want to, and the Holy Spirit will just stand by. He will be grieved, but He will not force you to do anything.

However, if you want to start living right, the Holy Spirit will help you. He will give you the ability to stop sinning if you want to. That is a part of His job.

All the things I have mentioned in this chapter are things God wants us to have and to do, to glorify Him in our lives. Proverbs 3:5 tells us, **Trust in the Lord with all your heart** [or spirit], **and lean not on your own understanding.** Jesus adds in John 4:24 that God is a Spirit. We should therefore not lean to our human ability to try to understand God but to our spirits and to His Word.

Jesus also says in John 4:24 that they who worship God must worship Him in spirit and in truth. Your mind and your spirit are two different things. That does not mean we should not use our minds, but it means we should use our spirits to worship God, as well as to understand the things of God.

We cannot worship God to our fullest potential unless we take full advantage of everything God has given us. That includes the gift of the Holy Spirit, with the evidence of speaking with tongues. Without that gift, we cannot do what God has commanded us to do — and John 4:24 is a commandment.

Being filled with the Spirit and speaking with other tongues is supposed to be the norm for Christians, just as it was for the people the book of Acts writes about. You do not need to be filled with the Spirit to be saved. However, the gift of the Holy Spirit empowers you. It will give you the power you need to really live that saved life to its fullest.

Lie 12
God Kills People

How many of us, at least in prior years, always thought God was the one who determined when people died? What I had envisioned was a great big tote board up in heaven, with everyone's names on it, and a red button by each name. That red button was the end-of-life button, and God would wake up every morning and say, "Gee, I wonder who I will zap out today?" If He pushed your button, that was it, you were dead. That is the idea people have of God, that He is the one who kills people.

Believe it or not, God has nothing to do with your dying. Nothing whatsoever. In fact, Jesus says in John 10:10 that He came that we might have life, and have it more abundantly. He also says several times in the four Gospels that He and His Father are one. If Jesus is giving us life, and God is giving us death, then something is thoroughly messed up.

In the first part of John 10:10, Jesus tells us exactly who is responsible for killing people, when He says, **"The thief does not come except to steal, and to kill, and to destroy."** If you have any doubts as to whom the thief is, notice what Paul says in Hebrews 2:9-15:

213

But we see Jesus, who was made a little lower than the angels, for the suffering of death crowned with glory and honor, that He, by the grace of God, might taste death for everyone.

For it was fitting for Him, for whom are all things and by whom are all things, in bringing many sons to glory, to make the captain of their salvation perfect through sufferings.

For both He who sanctifies and those who are sanctified are all of one, for which reason He is not ashamed to call them brethren,

saying,

"I will declare Your name to My brethren;

In the midst of the assembly I will sing praise to You."

And again:

"I will put my trust in Him."

And again:

"Here am I and the children whom God has given Me."

Inasmuch then as the children have partaken of flesh and blood, He Himself likewise shared in the same, that through death He might destroy him who had the power of death, that is, the devil,

and release them who through fear of death were all their lifetime subject to bondage.

These verses categorically prove that God is not the one killing people. Paul says in verse 14, **... that through death He might destroy him** [not an it — him] **who had the power** [or dominion] **of death.** He then clearly delineates who that person is, so we cannot mess it up — **the devil.**

See how slick the devil has been with these lies we have been pointing out? First, he gets you to believe there is no such thing as a personal devil. Then, when some calamity occurs, who do you have to blame? Certainly not the devil, because there is supposedly no such person. That leaves only God. That is why they call things like hurricanes, trees falling on houses and cars, floods and earthquakes "acts of God." They really should be called "acts of Satan."

Most people operate under the fear of death. They do not do many things, not because they do not really want to do them or do not really like them, but because they are afraid of dying from one of them. They say, "I'm afraid of water" or "I do not go swimming," but the real reason they do not do it is not because water has done anything to them. They do not go because of the fear of drowning, the fear of dying.

However, if you are a child of God, you really have nothing to be afraid of, as Paul points out in Hebrews 2:14:

> **Inasmuch then as the children have partaken of flesh and blood, He Himself likewise shared in the same, that through death He might destroy him who had the power of death, that is, the devil."**

The phrase **power of death** refers here to the dominion of death. According to Paul, Jesus took part of flesh and blood so that through death He **might destroy him who had the power** or authority over the dominion of death.

However, the word *destroy* in this verse does not mean "to put in a position of non-existence." When we think of something that is destroyed, we think of something that does not exist anymore. The word translated here as *destroy* does not mean that. What it means is "to render inoperative, to the point that it has no validity or power over you any longer."

That is what Paul means by destroy in Hebrews 2:14 — to limit the actions of the person who had the power of death, namely, the devil. Christ has destroyed the devil, or rendered him inoperative, as far as we are concerned.

At this point you may think, "All right, Brother Price, if God is not the person killing people, and the devil has no more legal authority to kill us, then who determines when we die?"

Are you ready for a shock? You do.

Hard-Pressed Between the Two

In Philippians 1:21, Paul says:

For to me, to live is Christ, and to die is gain.

That can sound like a strange statement. You may think, if that is all there is to life — to live out your whole life and come to the end and inherit a six-foot hole in the ground — and say, **For to me, to live is Christ, and to die is gain,** then dying has to be better than living to be a gain. If I have less as a result of dying, how can I gain?

What Paul means here is that Jesus is his reason for living. He is saying, "I am a child of God. I have been born of the Spirit of God. My life is the life of Christ. What I live now, I live by the Son of God. There is nothing else for me to live for."

However, that still does not answer the question of how Paul could say, **To die is gain.** I submit to you that for dying to be a gain, dying has to be better than living. There is no way it could be gain if it is the cessation of existence. If you cease to exist, there is no way dying can be a gain.

In the next few verses, Paul tells us how dying is a gain, and adds something that is nothing short of a hydrogen bomb when it comes to traditional church thinking on the subject.

Philippians 1:22-25:

> But if I live on in the flesh [or body], this will mean fruit from my labor; yet what I shall choose I cannot tell.
> For I am hard-pressed between the two, having a desire to depart and be with Christ, which is far better.
> Nevertheless to remain in the flesh is more needful for you.
> And being confident of this, I know that I shall remain and continue with you for all your progress and joy of faith.

Notice that Paul does not say in verse 22, "What God shall choose," "What Jesus shall choose," "What the Holy Spirit shall choose," or even "What Satan shall choose." He says, **What I shall choose.** It is Paul's choice, and the only way you can have a choice is if you have more than one thing to choose from. If you do not have anything to do with when you die, how can you be **hard-pressed between the two, having a desire to depart and be with Christ,** or to stay here in the flesh? You cannot. If you do not have any choice, you are not hard-pressed.

Many people end up dying in the prime of life because they think they are leaving when they die up to God, and are taking absolutely no control of the situation themselves. At the same time, God has left the situation in their hands, and is not touching it with a 29-$^1/_2$ foot pole. While they and God are waiting for one another, the devil comes in and kills them.

Satan is the author of death, not God. God did not kill any of your family, despite what the minister said at the time. If you decide to die, God will have to let you die — there is nothing He can do about it. We just read where Paul says, **I am hard-pressed between the two, having a desire to depart, to be with Christ.... Nevertheless to remain in the flesh is more needful for you.** He does not say God was in a strait, or the Holy Spirit, or Jesus. He says, **I am.**

"But brother Price, they killed Paul. They took him into custody and the Roman government killed him."

Not really. Paul allowed the Romans to use the method of decapitation as his exit from this world. He did not have to die that way.

If Paul had to die in captivity and had no other recourse, it invalidates the Bible. The Bible says God is no respecter of persons. He sent an angel down to a jail to let Peter out, and if He let Peter out and kept Paul in, He is a respecter of persons.

As far as I can tell, there is no biblical evidence that the church prayed for Paul to be released from jail. The Bible specifically says, however, that the church went into prayer for Peter, and that God sent an angel to let him out.

Just because a person is in the ministry, anointed by God, does not mean he knows everything. He can be just as wrong or ignorant about some things as everyone else. Paul was mightily used of God, but that does not mean he thought about everything. He might have accepted his lot in life. He obviously accepted his lot in life relative to being single. As far as we know, he did not get married after he got saved. He went through life without a wife. That was his choice, not God's.

The point is, a lot of the things we assume are God's choices are really ours. Because those choices are ours to make, there is nothing God can do about it. He let Paul stay in jail and He let Peter out, but Peter asked to get out. I have not found any evidence in my study of the Word that indicates Paul asked God to let him out.

If God wanted to make everything happen, He would have made you a robot. He would not have given you a free will. What good is it to give you a free will if God is going to make all the choices for you? If that were true, it would have been to God's benefit to make us robots. That way, He would never get any backtalk out of us. A robot never says, "Why me, Lord? What have I done to deserve this?" Only people do that.

With all this in mind, take a look at 1 Corinthians 3:18-23:

> Let no one deceive himself. If anyone among you seems to be wise in this age, let him become a fool, that he may become wise.

> For the wisdom of this world is foolishness with
> God. For it is written, "He catches the wise in their
> own craftiness";
> and again, "The Lord knows the thoughts of the
> wise, that they are futile."
> Therefore let no one boast in men. For all things
> are yours:
> whether Paul or Apollos or Cephas, or the world
> or life or death, or things present or things to come —
> all are yours.
> And you are Christ's, and Christ is God's.

Paul includes death as being yours. It is not up to
God or to the devil to determine when you are going to
die. It is up to you. You do not have to be a victim of the
circumstances. God has put you in control.

How Long Can We Live?

"Yeah, but Brother Price," you may think, "suppose the devil does not kill me. Suppose I live to be 90
years old. Do you mean I can just keep on living forever and ever?"

Not exactly. The physical world we live in now is
governed and influenced by sin, and everything in it is
working against you to destroy your flesh. The atmosphere itself will not let you live forever.

That does not mean you cannot live as long as you
want to within reason, however. The man says if you
dwell in the secret place of the Most High, and abide
under the shadow of the Almighty, that He will satisfy

you with long life and show you His salvation. You can stick around until you are satisfied, and if you are not satisfied, just keep on living.

God says in another scripture that the years of a man should be 120, so you can live to be at least 120 years old. Still another verse says the number of our days should be threescore and 10. One score is 10, three times 20 is 60, and 10 more is 70. That is the minimum number of years you should live, and you can go up to 120. I do not mean a feeble 120, with all your bodily functions dried up so you cannot enjoy life, your vision so dim that you bump into walls, or needing a cane or crutch to walk with, or riding around in a wheelchair. I am talking about living life at 120 with a spring in your step.

"But Brother Price, let's say I don't get sick, I don't drown, I don't die in an airplane crash or an accident. How am I eventually going to die?"

It is truly amazing how Christians have been lulled into thinking the only way to die is through sickness, disease, or some tragedy.

Have you ever considered the possibility of simply wearing out?

From a medical standpoint, we are all only a heartbeat away from death. All your heart has to do is stop, and you will not be around for long. God programmed it and it beats, day after day, hour after hour. Supposed it just stopped? I do not mean go in to a convulsion and have a coronary. I mean what if it just stopped beating?

The moment your heart stops, your spirit and soul leap out of your mouth and head for glory. You could be sitting in a chair at home when it happens, not hooked up to some respirator. You could be kicking back by the pool in your chaise lounge and just decide, "I think I'm going on to be with the Lord today."

In case you are wondering what the Bible says about this, take a look at Genesis 49:28-33, when Jacob blessed his 12 sons. Even though most of the scriptures in this book are from the New King James Version of the Bible, we will read these verses in Genesis and the scriptures on the next page from the original King James Bible.

> All these are the twelve tribes of Israel: and this is it that their father spake unto them, and blessed them; every one according to his blessing he blessed them.
>
> And he charged them, and said unto them, I am gathered unto my people: bury me with my fathers in the cave that is in the field of Ephron the Hittite,
>
> in the cave that is in the field of Machpelah, which is before Mamre, in the land of Canaan, which Abraham bought with the field of Ephron the Hittite for the possession of a buryingplace.
>
> There they buried Abraham and Sarah his wife; there they buried Isaac and Rebekah his wife; and there I buried Leah.
>
> The purchase of the field and of the cave that is therein was from the children of Heth.
>
> And when Jacob had made an end of commanding his sons, he gathered up his feet into the bed, and yielded up the ghost, and was gathered unto his people.

It implies here that Jacob chose his time to die. It does not say that death rushed in and took him away kicking and screaming. This was a volitional act on Jacob's part.

Also notice the term *yielded up the ghost* in verse 33.
There is one other, very important incident in the
Bible where that term is used — and it is reported in
virtually the same way in the original King James Bible
by four different people.

Luke 23:46, KJV:

And when Jesus had cried with a loud voice, he
said, Father, into thy hands I commend my spirit: and
having said thus, he gave up the ghost.

Mark 15:37, KJV:

And Jesus cried with a loud voice, and gave up
the ghost.

John 19:30, KJV:

When Jesus therefore had received the vinegar,
he said, It is finished: and he bowed his head, and
gave up the ghost.

Matthew 27:50, KJV:

Jesus, when he had cried again with a loud voice,
yielded up the ghost.

In each of these passages, it says that Jesus *gave up*
or *yielded up the ghost* — meaning that He voluntarily
gave up His life. That is what Jacob did, and it is what
you can do — after you have lived a long, healthy and
blessed life. There is no way you should allow death to
come in and take your life before you are ready.

"But Brother Price, what about the man who was killed in the airplane crash?" That is not important. You have no idea what that person believed, or whether or not he knew anything about the Word of God. The only thing that is important — the only thing God will hold you accountable for — is you.

Death — the Last Enemy

Because Adam sinned in the Garden of Eden, we have physical death in the world today. Because of this, everyone will eventually die physically, except for those people who are alive when Jesus returns. However, the Christian who is informed in the Word of God should see death simply as the means by which we transfer out of the physical realm into the spiritual realm. That person should have no fear or dread of death whatsoever.

This does not mean, by any stretch of the imagination, that physical death is our friend. In fact, Paul tells us in 1 Corinthians 15:21-26 that it is quite the opposite.

> For since by man came death, by Man also the resurrection of the dead.
> For as in Adam all die, even so in Christ shall all be made alive.
> But each one in his own order: Christ the firstfruits; afterward those who are Christ's at His coming.
> Then comes the end, when He delivers the kingdom to God the Father, when He puts an end to all rule and all authority and power.

God Kills People

> For He must reign, till He has put all enemies under His feet. The last enemy that will be destroyed is death.

There it is, in black and white: Death is our enemy. Normally, when an enemy attacks us, we protect ourselves and fight him off. That is exactly what we should do with death. We should bind it, rebuke it, resist it until we are ready to take our last breath — and that should not be until we are satisfied enough with a long life to want to move on.

Epilogue

The misconceptions we have covered in this book are by no means all the lies which Satan has attempted to pass off as genuine truths on the Body of Christ. The way you can tell what is the truth and what is not true is simple — check it out with the Word.

The Word of God is what you should use as a benchmark with which to measure any teaching or doctrine having to do with God. That is why God has made His Word so readily available to us. He wants us to check Him out.

Getting to know God to the best of our ability is something we should do every day — not just by reading the Bible, but studying it and getting to know the Word like we want to get to know God Himself. That is really what we are doing when we study His Word — we become familiar with God Himself and the way He operates in our lives. When we make searching out the things of God our primary goal in life, there will be no way the enemy can deceive us, and we can continually grow up in the things of God without missing so much as a step.

For a complete list of books and tapes by
Dr. Frederick K.C. Price, or to receive his publication,
Ever Increasing Faith Messenger, write

Dr. Fred Price
Crenshaw Christian Center
P.O. Box 90000
Los Angeles CA 90009

BOOKS BY FREDERICK K.C. PRICE, PH.D.

HIGH FINANCE
God's Financial Plan: Tithes and Offerings

HOW FAITH WORKS
(In English and Spanish)

IS HEALING FOR ALL?

HOW TO OBTAIN STRONG FAITH
Six Principles

NOW FAITH IS

THE HOLY SPIRIT —
The Missing Ingredient

FAITH, FOOLISHNESS, OR PRESUMPTION?

THANK GOD FOR EVERYTHING?

HOW TO BELIEVE GOD FOR A MATE

MARRIAGE AND THE FAMILY
Practical Insight for Family Living

LIVING IN THE REALM OF THE SPIRIT

THE ORIGIN OF SATAN

CONCERNING THEM WHICH ARE ASLEEP

HOMOSEXUALITY:
State of Birth or State of Mind?

PROSPERITY ON GOD'S TERMS

WALKING IN GOD'S WORD
Through His Promises

PRACTICAL SUGGESTIONS FOR SUCCESSFUL MINISTRY

NAME IT AND CLAIM IT!
The Power of Positive Confession

THE VICTORIOUS, OVERCOMING LIFE
(A Verse-by-Verse Study on the Book of Colossians)

A NEW LAW FOR A NEW PEOPLE

THE PROMISED LAND
(A New Era for the Body of Christ)

THREE KEYS TO POSITIVE CONFESSION

(continued on next page)

About the Author

Frederick K. C. Price, Ph.D., founded Crenshaw Christian Center in Los Angeles, California, in 1973, with a congregation of some 300 people. Today, the church's membership numbers well over 14,000 members of various racial backgrounds.

Crenshaw Christian Center, home of the renowned 10,146-seat FaithDome, has a staff of more than 200 employees. Included on its 30-acre grounds are a Ministry Training Institute, the Frederick K.C. Price III elementary and junior and senior high schools, as well as the FKCP III Child Care Center.

The *Ever Increasing Faith* television and radio broadcasts are outreaches of Crenshaw Christian Center. The television program is viewed on more than 100 stations throughout the United States and overseas. The radio program airs on over 40 stations across the country.

Dr. Price travels extensively, teaching on the Word of Faith simply and understandably in the power of the Holy Spirit. He is the author of several books on faith and divine healing.

In 1990, Dr. Price founded the Fellowship of Inner-City Word of Faith Ministries (FICWFM) for the purpose of fostering and spreading the faith message among independent ministries located in the urban, metropolitan areas of the United States.